In Kathryn's Korner

A Memoir

By Kathryn Spira

Zirlinson Publishing
2015

D1275706

In Kathryn's Korner

A Memoir

by
Kathryn Spira

As Told To Richard H. Nilsen

Edited by Shawn M. Tomlinson

ISBN: 978-1-329-70851-8

Cover photo by Erin Flynn

Zirlinson Publishing
Ballston Lake, New York
zirlinsonpublishing@gmail.com

In Kathryn's Korner

A Memoir

By Kathryn Spira

Zirlinson Publishing
2015

Acknowledgments

"The Hotel Denial" first appeared in Many Waters literary magazine at Empire State College in 2001 in a slightly altered form. I also have a bio, photos and brief write-up in ESC's alumni magazine 2002-2003.

New Mobility Magazine also published a version of "Hotel Denial" under their heading "My Spin" in February 2003 and some other autobiographical information in another issue published "Tales of Love and Terror" in the February 1999 issue about coping with MS and a relationship which appears here in altered form.

Some of the body of this book appeared first in The Sunday Leader-Herald, also in altered format over a period of 20 years from 1995 to 2015.

Illustrations from "The Book of Me" by Jacques Lorenzo (1988).

Recent photos by Richard Nilsen. Older photos from Erin Flynn of Los Angeles and various studios (head shots) and from various sources.

Contents

Author's Note

I've been writing a column for our local daily newspaper in Upstate New York for the Sunday edition for more than 20 years.

It was never my goal to be a newspaper columnist.

I wanted to be an actress or maybe sing and dance on stage.

But along the way to my dream, I was diagnosed with MS.

I can tell you that this diagnosis has turned into a gift that changed my perspective on life and what was important.

Along the way, many people have been helpful, caring, loving and supportive.

This book of my memoirs is a culmination of my experiences as well as a tribute to all those people, family and friends who have helped me along the way.

This support has been overwhelming.

I have so much to say and share due to all these people who have been in my, that is, In Kathryn's Korner!

Many of the columns I have written for The Sunday Leader-Herald over the years may be accessed at its website www.leaderherald.com or at my own website www.kathrynskorner.com

— Kathryn Spira
Nov. 18, 2015
Caroga Lake, NY

A Note From 'Herman'

Although referred to as "Herman" in her weekly column, there is truth in that I have been "her man" as well as being in Kathryn's corner for more than two decades.

You could say we came upon each other late in life. I had a previous marriage and three, now grown, children and she had been pursuing her dream of acting when she was struck down with MS.

As the MS has progressed, I often have been Kathryn's arms and legs and even her spokesman when speech becomes difficult.

Her constant optimism and lack of complaints in the face of a debilitating, chronic condition has been an inspiration to her readers, family, friends and admirers.

I often say to those meeting her for the first time that the Kathryn they meet in the first five minutes is the real Kathryn. There are no onion layers to peel back to get to the person underneath.

She has been a constant joy, even when being a pain in the butt.

In the best of ways, Kathryn has never grown up. She has a childlike wonder and openness that is rare in one who has seen as much of the world as she has.

In a world of fakery, pretense and role playing, Kathryn is the real deal.

I stand solidly In Kathryn's Korner.

— Richard Nilsen
Nov. 12, 2015
Caroga Lake, NY

A Note From the Editor

I started writing the Hitchhiker in Time columns for The Sunday Leader-Herald — my second run at the column after it first appeared in The ECHO almost a decade before — when Kathryn Spira came to my attention.

It actually was at a going-away party for someone from The Leader-Herald at the former Milt Schaber's restaurant in Gloversville, NY, probably in 1994.

Kathryn was sitting across the restaurant with someone I don't recall, and she was pointed out to me as the columnist behind Kathryn's Korner.

I would be lying if I said I "loved" Kathryn's Korner from the beginning. I was young and had very specific ideas of what a column should be.

Ah well, I thought. She writes what she writes, I write what I write and never the twain shall meet.

Then, I met her again at one of Richard Nilsen's writers' groups and, well, I liked her.

It wasn't long before the two of them were "an item," and I saw a bit more of her occasionally. Richard was in love with her and he was my friend, so I wished them all the best.

I did not realize until she later told me that I "outed" her about her MS in my Hitchhiker in Time column, and I felt terrible about it. I didn't do it on purpose. I simply thought it was common knowledge.

Then, I went back to work at The Leader-Herald, this time as the Sunday editor. Kathryn still was writing her column and now it was my time to edit it weekly.

I know that up to that point, she had a big following, but my problem with her column at that point was that the columns didn't really seem to be about much except her daily musings.

This seemed ridiculous, I thought, considering how interesting her background was, and how interested readers would be to read the anecdotal stories of her time as an actress.

I conveyed this thought to Richard and to my managing editor, and we all agreed the column could be much better than it was.

And soon, it was.

Kathryn started telling stories about Hollywood, her actor friends, her unique experience.

Kathryn Spira has had an interesting, unusual life. Some of that has been not so good because of her MS. Some of it — her acting days and her days with Richard — has been unlike anything else.

The best thing for me as her friend is that she pulls no punches and has no problem in person saying to people to their faces some pretty sobering things.

How can you not love that?

— Shawn M. Tomlinson
Nov. 18, 2015
Ballston Lake, NY

In Kathryn's Korner

A Memoir

By Kathryn Spira

Zirlinson Publishing
2015

This is me standing on the balcony of a hotel overlooking
Alexandria Bay in 1995.

Chapter 1

The Hotel Denial

Name's Kathryn.

Game's Humor.

Disability's MS.

It's not what I'm about, (the MS, I mean), just thought I'd get the details out of the way. (Now you just relax. If you don't find that my game is humor, just bear with me anyway. I write a weekly column, which both myself and some readers find amusing.)

Well educated, studied the arts in college, opera, theater, and dance.

Decided to let the rest of the world in on my little secret, and moved to New York City. Worked in the theater there, went to some of the best acting schools there, and subsequently became one of the very best waitresses there.

With, of course, zero money.

But all in the name of the arts, there was no self-doubt, or hesitation, struggling was necessary for the greatness that was lurking just ahead.

In the meantime, I was becoming an extraordinarily

proficient waitress.

Hooked up with a barrage of ridiculous men, all of whom had no jobs, money, or ambition, and I knew I could help them. (Co-dependent was not yet a buzzword).

Let me just fast-forward, before this becomes akin to *The Days of Wine and Roses*.

Was doing a play in New York, off-off Broadway. (I had convinced myself that this was an "important piece," and part of my dues-paying.) It was OK that I wasn't being paid, (again), all in the name of art, thus making the big payola even more sweet, when it did happen.

And I *knew* it would.

I've always said that 'Denial' is a great place to go. Free rooms, and never a problem with reservations.

Three weeks into the run, the director, (also unpaid, and waiting for his 'big' break), pulls me aside, and asks me, in a stage whisper, if I have some type of personal problem that I feel like sharing with him.

Oh, the eighties, and the introduction of all that new age jargon!

I'm like, "What's up? Cuz, if you're cruising to sleep with me, this pseudo-sensitive crap is so the wrong approach." "Plus," I continued, "I totally had written you off as gay. And I consider myself an excellent judge." "Kathryn," he impatiently replied,

be tapping, "yes, I am gay, thank-
t the point. What I'm speaking of is
't understand a word you're saying
can't, that means the audience can't

at deductive reasoning. What's your

f speaking to a child, he says, "If
me type of problem, and you must
For goodness sakes', there's no
ourself in alcohol. There, I've said

Stunned, but still able to speak, I sputter, "What are you talking about?"

I honestly hadn't a clue what he was speaking of.

"OK, Kathryn, we'll play it your way," he said.

Then, "Why don't you tell me why your speech is so slurred."

Still sparring, I say, "Yeah, well, how can you understand me now?"

He replies, "I'm standing right in front of you, and concentrating very hard."

I have no reply, but I still parry with, "Yeah, s-so?" (very close to tears, lower lip quivering.)

Thus began my journey years ago into the as-yet-un-sailed waters in which I am now a seasoned sailor.

Started with a hearing exam, as all hearing on the

right side was missing.

I assumed this is why I was speaking "funny." This was particularly festive, the highlight being when I flipped out, pounding on the glass walls of the cubicle they put me in for the test.

Thing is, you are put into a soundproof box, given headphones, so the only thing you can hear is what the person testing you is saying.

OK. So begins my test.

I'm trying to remain calm, (a big job), my best friend Jacques, (who is sadly no longer with us), is there for support.

Armed, of course, with a jumbo box of Puffs — treated with aloe for sensitive noses — and, of course, bottled water.

Jacques' famous credo, (one of many), was to always replenish tears with drinking water. As I had been crying for weeks, this was a good move, both with the water and the Puffs.

So into the glass chamber I go, grinning courageously. I can see the guy who is about to test me and my ears. He gives me the pre-arranged thumbs up sign, indicating testing is about to begin.

Roger.

I shoot back thumbs up, smile, all systems go. Over and out. I'm ready to rock, and kick this hearing test in the butt. I see the testers' mouth moving, and hear nothing.

All bravado fizzles, and I become an insane person. Think Dustin Hoffman in *The Graduate* in the scene where he's trying with everything in him to get into the church, (the climax being when he is up on the window, Christ style), you get the idea.

I'm banging on the windows, crying with real tears, and absolutely convinced that I am now deaf. The hearing tester-person gets on the headphones, and says, (which I can hear), very self-deprecatingly, "Heh-heh. Sorry, I forgot to turn on the sound."

I am so not amused, but at the same time so very pleased that I can hear, that I recover beautifully, and say, "I'm cool. That's fine."

How'd this guy get this job??!

Passed the hearing test, went through every other test available to eliminate other illnesses, finally was sent to a neurologist who was able to diagnose "possible" MS. At that point, I was ready to throw a cocktail party just for finally knowing.

In the same vein, I was like, no way. These guys are so wrong.

So wrong, that they are on the near side of being right.

Morons. Afraid of malpractice. Probably did some bad drugs in the sixties, to boot, and are really paranoid. So my right leg is dragging. So what!!

Duh! It's clearly a sports injury, (I was doing a lot of working out, and running at the time).

I do some research myself, and find that most people are not diagnosed with MS, (which *I did not have*) 'til their late 20s, or 30s, or later.

I mean, I'm not a rocket scientist, but, hello! I'm only 23. (Check here my denial reference). Ten full years, of what I now know as remission, further convinces me of the doctor's stupidity.

Fast forward 10 and a half years, and I'm living in LA. with, yet another ridiculous man, (co-dependant was a buzz word. I was choosing to ignore it).

Still looking for fame, and, (sigh), love.

Damn "sports injury" comes back, and my right leg is dragging, big time. After much vacillating, go to see a sports medicine doctor, and convince myself it's bursitis, (again, check here again for my denial reference).

Finally, I am sent to a, (dammit), "N" word, (I could not bring myself to say the word neurologist).

Ya know what, at present, it's three decades later, and, yep, it is MS. And yep, it does suck.

But not all the time, and not nearly as heinously as I had anticipated. It's not what I'm about. (I know I've said that twice, but I mean business!)

I have a completely new perspective on life, and am, (irritatingly), happy. Not chemically induced either. I've always been very upbeat, and though this is a tough nut to crack, as it were, plow on do I.

The MS helped emancipate me from all the "glory" in Hollyweird, (my name, and trust me, very accurate), as I finally made a pact with myself to eliminate all those things that did not make me happy. Loved acting, it was the 'scene' in LA that made me nuts.

Too much posturing, lying, games, etc.

Not the reason I wanted to go in to the business, or stay in it.

This was taken by my adoptive father, Joe Spira, in my high school production of *The Music Man* with me as Marion the Librarian in 1977.

Chapter 2

'The Music Man'

And now I want to go back in time.

My "career," as it were, began in my junior year of high school at Cleveland Heights High School.

The director of the Girl's Glee Club/Men's Chorus, Bill Thomas, was auditioning for the musical *The Music Man*. It was my very first audition with, I think, five other girls competing for the part. Much to my surprise and delight I was cast as Marion the Librarian, the female lead. As I recall the director, Bill Thomas, pretty much had me in mind since he knew me from Girl's Glee Club.

I had been a member of the chorus, but never tried acting as well as singing in any capacity before.

My parents came to every performance, with my step-dad armed with a video camera, which he never quite mastered, so there is no record of what transpired. In my mind and the cast and audience memories, the play was a success with me getting my first taste of "the acting buzz" of an audience clapping ferociously.

That was in 1977.

As I was going through old photos, I came upon a picture taken of me singing "My White Knight."

I remember the director, Bill Thomas, changed the lyrics to "My Bright Knight," so it wouldn't seem to have any racial connotation since our high school was interracial with about half and half black and white student body.

In the picture I am wearing a high-collar, long cotton print dress that came from the wardrobe department, something I never would have had in my closet. I'm sitting on the front porch of my parent's home supposedly dreaming about my co-star Harold Hill (played by Michael Oster, incidentally my first gay leading man who was quite a character and had bad breath which I remember with horror from our kissing scenes). Oster had a beautiful voice which I especially remember from his rendition of the memorable song from the musical, *Seventy-six Trombones.*

My best friend from high school, Carol Gifford, was in the next musical I was in called *How to Succeed in Business Without Really Trying*, where I played Miss Jones and she played Miss Krump. I remember Carol singing "This Irresistible Paris Original" about a dress and I remember we both laughed so hard she could barely get through the song. I also sang a finalé of a song called "The Brotherhood of Man," Pierpont Finch (most recently played on Broadway by Daniel Radcliffe of Harry Potter fame) was singing along with the men's chorus where I had to jump up on a desk and belt out the tune with the lyrics,

Oh, that noble feeling, Feels like bells are pealing, Down with double-dealing, Oh Brother! You, you got me; Me, I got you, you!

One thing I learned about acting in my first musical was how to seem romantically involved with a gay man with bad breath! (Also, my character as Marion was very different from my personality in *The Music Man*.)

I remember they wanted me to wear wire-rimmed glasses, which I refused and that was the first in a long line of stubborn decisions which probably did my career no good, in that I later refused to appear in a movie scene (*One Woman, Or Two*) with Nick Nolte, which may have advanced my career, but I refused because I would have to appear in the nude and didn't want my first impression on the public to be that. My theatrical agent, Tom Jennings, was really mad at me when I turned it down.

Anyway, when I watched an episode of the TV show *Glee!* A few years ago, it was about putting on the musical *West Side Story*, and it brought back a flood of memories.

When I was in the Girl's Glee Club/Men's Chorus in Cleveland Heights High School, we did a production of *West Side Story* that I was in as the character Consuelo, one of the Shark girls.

I wanted to play the role of Maria so badly, but I was happy to be cast in the musical at all. Our production was choreographed with dancing as well as singing, so it was a fairly complicated production for a high school group to put on.

Our production certainly paled by comparison to that put on the TV show *Glee*, but then I don't think any high school group can compare to the professional caliber of singers and dancers on *Glee*.

And remember, for TV, they can keep doing takes until its perfect.

Bottom line is this: The actors portraying high school students in *Glee* seem like they are way more professional than any high school group could ever be. I doubt any high school glee club director looks at *Glee* and says, "Yeah, we could do that!"

Actually, my high school classmate Sean Young was also in the production. I can't remember who she played, but she did go on to play many movie and TV parts later, such as co-starring with Darryl Hannah and Harrison Ford in *Blade Runner*.

It's funny, I don't remember her character in the play and she didn't strike me as particularly memorable back then. I know I was thrilled to be in the musical but I don't remember much else about it. But the episode of *Glee* brought back memories of *West Side Story* and how thrilled I was to be a part of such a production.

This was my first contact sheet of head shots taken by a studio in Cleveland when I was about 15 in 1975.

Chapter 3

Off to College

After high school, I received an opera scholarship, of all things, when my guidance counselor suggested I apply at Indiana University School of Music.

Let's face it, no one was applying for opera scholarships in Cleveland during the 1970s, so there was less competition for the money.

So, off to I.U. I went, where I first studied under Roy Samuelson, an opera coach and I have to admit I hated it! My memories of Roy came back after watching a *Holiday on Ice* TV show with classical music accompaniment.

The soprano that the cameras dwelled upon was particularly wrong for this venue. There were operatic high notes held over-long for pop songs that didn't lend themselves to operatic trills.

When I went to Indiana University, I was paired off with Samuelson, who I didn't care for at all because he liked that kind of operatic seriousness that fosters expressions like, "It ain't over until the fat lady sings."

I was wandering the halls at I.U. School of Music and happened upon an office door that had a floor-to-sill poster that read, "Opera sucks!" I was so enamored with the sign that I knocked on the door and noticed at that time there was a smaller sign that said, "Eileen Farrell."

That prompted me to knock and be greeted by a warm smile from the singer Eileen Farrell, who took me under her wing and taught me to sing jazz and scat, something she chose to focus on with successful recordings and concerts to back it up.

What a thrill for me to get to know her not realizing she was well known for her singing. I think she liked the fact that I happened to knock on her door and wasn't one of those who lined up to be in her classes and wasn't impressed by her fame.

Yup, you guessed it. She was to be my opera voice coach. And here's what I learned about her in talking to her. I was amazed that she was actually in and invited me in as well. I immediately asked what was up with the sign if she was an opera voice coach. She very simply said, "The sign says it all. Been there, done that."

Even though she had recorded several successful opera albums, her first love was singing blues and jazz. And she had a special gift with scat singing, where the singer makes up nonsensical words and sounds to go with the music.

I remember doing a duet with Eileen of "The Man I Love" on the main stage at the School of Music at I.U. in the late 1970s. The performance was part of a master class in music, kind of a final exam in performance. Performing with her on stage as part of a master class was a great thrill for me because she was so down-to-earth and unaffected by her fame.

I had gone to I.U. on an opera scholarship and Farrell had earned her early reputation in opera, but just as she changed her focus to blues and jazz, she also influenced me to focus more on popular blues and jazz singing.

I happened to see a You Tube video recording of Farrell being interviewed by Charlie Rose and one of the things she spoke of was how important the words and lyrics of songs were to her. She said while teaching at I.U., her best students were from the theater department rather than voice training because theater people understood the importance of the meaning of words. That was something she stressed in her classes.

Even though I went on to pursue acting rather than singing, Farrell had a strong influence on me and I know I always thought about the importance of words, meaning and what they conveyed to the audience.

As Farrell said in her interview with Rose, so many modern singers don't convey the meaning of the lyrics and are hard to understand because that isn't their main concern.

The meanings of words were important to Farrell and they are to me, too.

It's ironic that scat singing, where words and sounds are made up to accompany the music, was also an important part of Farrell's repertoire. But then again, since scat words are culled from the emotional content of the music, it lends itself to a fuller interpretation of the music.

Between semesters, I continued to pursue my acting experiences through summer stock and regional theaters near my home in Cleveland at Cain Park Summer Theater in Cleveland and Chagrin Valley Little Theater in Chagrin Falls, a beautiful bedroom community outside of Cleveland.

My next acting experience was at Cain Park Summer Theatre in Cleveland in the play *A Member of the Wedding*, where I was cast as Janice, sister of the bride. I remember as Janice I had to play up a "tomboy" persona, which really was acting because I did not grow up as a tomboy.

It was also my first drama and the first time I ever performed in an amphitheater (outdoors). That means it was cold in the evening performances and afternoon performances were bug-filled and sometimes too warm, especially for an active part on stage.

The next theater experience I had of any note was with the Phoenix Theatre Ensemble in Cleveland where I met my friend Raj Bahadur who I not only still email back and forth with, but who has also contributed to my columns over the years.

With Phoenix I played Portia in Shakespeare's *Merchant of Venice*, which was my first classical acting part. I remember the iambic pentameter of Shakespeare's language was especially difficult to grasp and perform. But it was all in the name of art, growing as an actress and advancing my budding career goals.

This photo of the ART Reach production of *Hansel and Gretel* was likely taken by Kathryn Schultz Miller, the playwright and director, and shows me as the wicked witch and Dahn Schwartz as Hansel.

Chapter 4

Off to Tour With ART Reach

I wound up leaving I.U. at the end of my junior year because I got hired to tour with the American Repertory Theater's outreach program called "ART Reach."

It came about like this. Kathryn Schultz Miller and her husband Barry came to the theater department at I.U. looking for actors to take part in their upcoming tour.

Kathryn was my first acting employer and I had a chance to interview her a few years back for my columns and she graciously replied to my questions. This was the same time I started waitressing and since we never stayed out over night, I was able to tour with ART Reach by day and waitress at night at Flannigan's Landing in Cincinnati on the waterfront.

I had a blast at Flannigan's. I would carry a full tray of cocktails over my head through the packed bar because the place was so crowded everybody couldn't get up to the bar itself.

Plus, since the waitress got the drinks for the standing patrons as well as collect bartabs, I had to hold the tray of drinks over my head with my left hand and hold the cash between my first two fingers in that same hand while I dispensed the drinks with my right hand. It was a big party atmosphere and got my adrenaline going after being on the road all day with ART Reach.

I made a lot of money because there was no space to make change so people just automatically gave the next higher denomination for every drink. I made at least "100 beans" as we said back then in tips every night, which was pretty good for those days.

ART Reach had both a full-time cast and a part-time cast. The full-time cast toured the tri-state Ohio-Indiana-Kentucky area schools while as I recall, the part-time cast played occasional gigs at schools in the immediate Cincinnati area.

This is part of an interview I had with Miller about her career as playwright, artistic director, publisher and marketer of her 56 original plays.

So it was in my third year at Indiana University that there was a call notice for auditions for ART Reach. Upon reading further I understood it was a children's touring theatre company which was a part of the American Repertory Theatre.

I had never done nor was familiar with children's theater, but I knew from the description it was to be for school aged children and we would be performing in the auditorium of each school we were assigned to.

I remember the children being absolutely mesmerized at the idea of live theater being presented by an acting troupe coming to the school to perform. It must have been a combination of real live actors performing in a sort of fantasy way for these kids.

The picture at this chapter's beginning is of Hansel and Gretel with me playing the witch handing a pie through the window to Hansel. I am sure you are all familiar with the storyline.

In the picture I am handing the pie to actor Dahn Schwartz, portraying Hansel. The girl who played Gretel was my friend Tracey Huffman. We became great buddies throughout the tour but I have pretty much lost contact with her over the years. The fourth person in the acting troupe was named John and for the life of me I cannot remember his last name, this is perhaps because he was not a very nice person and the rest of us couldn't stand him. Now keep in mind we are traveling in a big bright red and white van with the name "ART Reach" printed on the side of the van prominently.

Keep in mind we were traveling in close quarters with meals and lodging paid for by the directors, and when I say lodging I specifically remember the four of us crashing on someone's living room floor somewhere in Indiana, so it was not all that glamorous.

I also remember staying at hotels, but they were far and few between. We were mostly put up at the friends of the directors' houses on the road.

I emailed the artistic director of the troupe asking her the last name of the actor John, who I distinctly remember as John "something." I didn't have fond memories of him, nor I imagine him of me.

She immediately emailed me back and said, "It was Kathryn Joan P. Andrew Spira, Tracey Andrew Huffman, Dahn Andrew Schwarz and John Andrew White! Sometimes you would all introduce yourselves that way to get John Andrew White's goat."

We couldn't stand him, especially having to be with him 24/7!

ART Reach was basically an outreach program to children in elementary school, and I would like to think that it made a lasting impression on them.

At the audition for the job, I met Miller, and read for her from a piece she gave out. Kathryn was very bubbly, funny, smiley and very encouraging to an actor just starting her career. I've always known her as Kathryn (same spelling as my name) but she refers to herself now as Kathy, which I will do as well to keep from confusing interviewer and interviewee.

Here's a short bio: Kathy co-founded the professional ART Reach Touring Theatre and served as Artistic Director for more than 20 years. Most of her 56 plays have been published and have won countless awards. Her play *A Thousand Cranes* was performed at the Kennedy Center, the Sundance Institute, and has been produced thousands of times the world over. She has won playwriting fellowships from the National Endowment for the Arts, the Ohio Arts Council and the Post-Corbett Foundation. Kathy lives in Cincinnati with her husband Barry, who handles orders, soundtracks and website design for ART Reach Children's Theatre Plays.com.

Kathryn: How did ART Reach Touring Theatre get started?

Kathy: I always did theatre in High School with Young People's Theatre in Cincinnati. In college many of my friends from those days got together and started American Repertory Theatre (ART). We had three projects, Shakespeare in the Park, a Main Stage Children's Theatre program and a program that took shows to schools. While there had been a lot of government funding for the arts for years, that was suddenly pulled and many arts companies across the country closed up or reorganized. ART broke up, Shakespeare folded, a friend took the Main Stage and I took ART Reach. I felt ART Reach was the best bet because it could bring in its own income from the schools and did not require maintenance of a building. And I was right, at its height the company had a budget of half a million dollars while many other theatre ventures failed.

Kathryn: How did you come to Indiana University to recruit? (Because that's where I auditioned for it and was hired. I think that audition was in 1981.) As a side note I will tell you that because of this job, I didn't finish college at the time, although I did complete the degree in 2001 at Empire State College where I'm happy to say all my credits matriculated.

Kathy: Congratulations on the degree. I had no idea you put off school for ART Reach! (Hmm, not sure if I would have suggested you do that.) We went to a lot of effort to get good actors. You really can't just put an ad in the paper and expect you'll find enough people in Cincinnati. Each state usually has auditions, mostly kids graduating that year from college. And then there are regionals such as the Southeastern Theatre Conference. We went to all of those looking for the best. You were one of them!

Kathryn: What were the nuts and bolts to

organizing and running ART Reach?

Kathy: Unlike many theatre people, I really enjoyed the business aspect of it. I put a lot of emphasis on booking a full calendar. We went to two schools a day and did as many as three shows a day. It was hard work but we booked that calendar five days a week for nine months every year. We did literally thousands of performances a year. There's a lot of strategy that goes into plotting the route and itinerary to make it all run smoothly.

Kathryn: And there's a lot of work that goes into setting up, performing and driving from school to school for two or three shows a day!

Kathy: The most difficult aspect of it for me was personnel. It's difficult to get young actors to commit for nine months to a strenuous tour. Many loved the idea of "winning" at auditions but simply didn't like the real hard work of touring. Many actors think doing children's theatre is beneath them, so you have to always try to convince them that the work is important. (By the way I think this attitude has changed quite a bit over the years.) It was hard to find people who really loved the work and did a great job. That said, I always felt our success was due to the wonderful work of the extremely talented actors who did work hard and did do a terrific job.

Kathryn: How big of a role did Barry have in it?

Kathy: I met Barry through the friends I had at Young People's Theatre. We actually started ART together with three other friends. Barry was President of ART at its inception. A year later we got married, not long after that we put all our efforts behind ART Reach. I guess you could say we were a husband and wife team, I was Artistic Director but his involvement was equal to mine.

Kathryn: In comparison, what is ART Reach today? Is it still going strong? Are you going to be handing it on to someone else?

Kathy: By 1996, I had been with the company for 20 years, most of that time running it myself. I felt it was time to move on. I turned the reins over to a similar company from Richmond VA, Theatre IV. I have to say I was not that happy with how they handled the company, so I was glad when Theatre IV gave it up after about six years and ART Reach became a program under the Cincinnati Children's Theatre. Kelly Germain engineered all that, she's Artistic Director, and I have great confidence in her (she started as an actor in the company and directed shows for me). Under Kelly's leadership the company has done well.

Kathryn: What are you doing differently today?

Kathy: I now run an Internet publishing company called ART Reach Children's Theatre Plays which is quite successful. On my website I sell scripts and licensing for all the plays I wrote for ART Reach Touring Theatre. I have also written many, many more plays. So many I don't know the exact count, but it's around 60 plays. We have thousands of producers around the world. Barry and I work together. We have no other jobs and no other employees. Its wonderful, rewarding work and we couldn't hope for more success or happiness!

Kathryn: Have you any amusing anecdotes like your reminder how we used to introduce ourselves?

Kathy: Well, don't you remember my friend Fran's niece? This was during the very early years, in 1983, we went to a national conference in Minneapolis to perform Blue Horses (which got a standing ovation, by the way). A friend of mine said her niece would be happy to have us stay at her house. Let's just say they really didn't want us to stay there. They led us past bedrooms and couches to a very hot windowless room with nothing in it but a hard floor. I guess they thought we'd sleep on the floor. Anyway we took one look at the room (suitcases in our hands) and tried to hem-haw our way out of it. We had to thank them very kindly but maneuver ourselves out of there. You, dear Kathryn, kept saying "I'll pay for a hotel!! I'll pay, I'll pay!!!" We did find a hotel room that seemed like heaven after the prospect of a night in Hades. We all went out to eat that night and sat around a table laughing until there were tears in our eyes! It's one of my most fun memories.

Kathryn: And did I actually pay for the hotel? I know I've been famous for offering to pay these days and not following through!

Kathy: I don't think you did pay. However, you always seemed to have more money than anyone else those days.

Kathryn: (That's because Mom and Dad couldn't bear to think of me as a starving artist. They always came to my rescue and were my biggest supporters and fans. Also, I waitressed nights when we were in town.)

Back in 2009 I remember watching the Tony Awards. I awaited this awards show with great anticipation, not because I was familiar with any of the Broadway musicals or plays being nominated, but I am familiar with many of the actors that played in them.

When the first award was given to Scarlett Johansson for best featured actress and she thanked Greg Mosher for telling her she could do what she didn't think she could, I remember thinking at the time, "I don't remember how or from when, but I remember the name Greg Mosher."

As if she were reading my mind, I got an email

from Kathryn Schultz Miller:

"Did you know that you met Gregory Mosher (up for Tony tonight) while touring with ART Reach? It was 1982-83 and he was reporting for the National Endowment for the Arts. He took us all out for a drink after a performance of 'Blue Horses.' He liked YOU! Later married oh, what's her name, Isabella Rosselini? Ingrid Bergman's daughter. Then divorced. Just thought you might enjoy that angle."

As with many of my male pursuits, especially in the 80s, this one escaped me. I just don't remember him at all, and when I saw him on the Tonys, well it WAS 30 years later, I just didn't recognize him as he is bald as an eagle.

I did look him up and found out: "Gregory Mosher is a theatre director who is presently a professor of theatre at Columbia University and director of Columbia's Arts Initiative. He is a Tony Award-winning director and producer of nearly two hundred stage productions – at the Lincoln Center and Goodman Theatres, on and off-Broadway, at the Royal National Theatre, and in the West End. He is also a film and television director, producer, and writer."

I feel kind of ridiculous now for not being able to remember him. At the time, I guess he was reviewing us for a grant for the NEA, and I guess he just didn't make an impression on me-what can I say?

It's funny, one of my readers named Nancy often comments how she is surprised what a good memory I have and in this case my memory fails me. I remember his name but not the experience.

So I emailed Kathy back and asked if she remembered any of the details of Greg liking *me* and whether or not I responded. I just couldn't remember. She wrote back in her typical tongue-in-cheek humor:

"Yeah, well you attracted men like flies, I don't think you could remember every fly.

He wasn't exactly hitting on you but I don't think he'd have taken us out for a drink if it weren't for you. He clearly had eyes for you.

I was ticked because having these big shots come in was quite a lot of nerve-wracking trouble for me. Not only did I have to pick their cheap butts up at the airport but I had to suffer being the low life children's theatre person while they talked about off-Broadway and all I stood to get from NEA was $5,000.

He wore a beret because he was balding and lots of pins on his backpack to prove he'd been around. It was a few years later he married Isabella Rosselini.

They divorced soon after that.

I couldn't believe it. But he hasn't gone away. There he was on the Tonys."

And was there any more to the story?

Kathy followed up with: "Oh, and he did tell you call him when you were in New York. I remember that very well, he gave you the name of his agent."

The agent apparently didn't do me any good. I went through a lot of episodes trying to get an agent. But still, since he had gone to that trouble, I had to try and remember.

So I did a freeze-frame on Greg's face with our DVR when the camera showed him in the crowd as Scarlett was heaping thanks on him. I looked a long time. But nope, still can't place him.

My ART Reach experience was a good "training in the trenches" before trying New York City's Off Broadway venue, which was very difficult to break into.

KATHRYN J. SPIRA

This "serious" head shot of me was likely taken by a studio in New York City in the late 1980s.

Chapter 5

Off to Off Off Broadway

From the proceeds of waitressing and ART Reach, I was able to buy a 1972 VW, Kelly-green square back I named Otto the Auto. (It was actually my second car after a 1966 VW orange bug that had racing stripes, chrome bumpers and a passenger side "kill switch" behind the seat to keep it from being stolen.)

Otto was my transport to New York City, the Big Apple where I was going to make my name and fortune!

But as always, I spent a lot of time driving Otto to the Hamptons to be at the beach and visit my sister's family. The beach has always been a distraction for me in pursuing my career!

After my year with ART Reach, I wanted to pursue my professional career and it seemed like no place could be better for that than New York City.

I was walking down Broadway and bumped into Cindy Dutton on the corner of 57th Street and Eighth Avenue. Trouble was, when I went to NYC, I didn't have a place to live when I got there.

As I struck up a conversation with Cindy, I found she was also an aspiring actress and living alone in a studio apartment. She very graciously offered to let me stay with her until I found my own place.

Cindy's sister, Stacey Dutton was also living in an apartment in NYC and also an aspiring actress and agent (who later became a successful agent for Bon Jovi). I met Stacey through her sister Cindy and became friends with both these wonderful ladies.

Imagine taking someone off the street you had just met into your home! I was so grateful and still am.

Cindy, Stacey and I all took jobs working in restaurants until our "big breaks" came along. With Stacey, that would be as a successful casting director, producer and actress as well as an agent for Bon Jovi and other entertainment venues.

As I recall, Cindy got married without furthering an entertainment career like her sister. Stacey worked at "Formerly Joe's" with me in New York City and I believe Cindy was bar-tending at "Amy's Pub" at that time. Amy's was on 8th Avenue in Hell's Kitchen at that time, the neighborhood where I got my own apartment after I started working. Come to think of it, Cindy got me my first job bartending at Amy's before I went to work at Formerly Joe's.

When Stacey's birthday reminder recently popped up on my Facebook page, I wished her the best and she immediately replied with thanks and her love. Good to be reminded after all these years that there are still some great people in the entertainment industry. I even got to see her host the reality show "Clean Sweep" on cable awhile back.

NYC was where I first went to a professional acting school--my first training since my days as an acting student at Indiana University. This was when I was first introduced to "method acting" at Theater In Action on 14th Street in a warehouse in the meat packing district.

My teacher's name was Lev Schectman who came to New York by way of Russia. He ascribed to the techniques taught by the great Constantin Stanislavski and brought those theories to the acting troup he named Theater in Action.

What was weird about going to that studio for my weekly studies was that there was always a pervasive smell of dead animals as it had been a working meat packing plant. (It was ironic that we would go from the meat packing plant to "cattle calls" for auditions with lots of competition for roles.)

I was unsuccessful at getting an agent in New York City, so every Wednesday along with the thousands of unemployed actors I would pick up a copy of "Back Stage" which had all the auditions listed for the week including mostly off Broadway stuff.

It was from there that I got my first jobs as an actor in what is known as off-off Broadway. They were basically very small theaters off the beaten track which were unpaid and poorly attended.

This takes me into my 30s when I met my then boyfriend Brad and we did a play together. I met him doing *Getting Out of Bed*, which was an off-off Broadway play. From there his career was taking off and he got a job in a new pilot called *Mulberry Street* which was shooting in Los Angeles.

This is how I got to California as I moved out there with him. The show was supposed to be picked up by a network and it seemed like a good time for both of us to move.

Alas, the show was never picked up and Brad and I never worked out either. I chose to stay out in Los Angeles and pursue my career there. However, one good thing that did come out of this experience was that at the filming of the pilot, I met my first agent, Tom Jennings.

But back to New York City, where it took me a full year to get my first part onstage.

The venue at the American Renaissance Theatre was considered off-off Broadway and it was unpaid. Off-Broadway casting directors looking for new talent were often invited to attend as they were as anxious to find new talent as we were to break into the business.

My first role was as Cheryl in *Sisters of Sisters*, a story that portrayed four sisters and their families.

I met a lot of people in the entertainment business from this part and the production ran for three months.

The theatre was on Hudson Street and I was living in Greenwich Village at the time. I remember my mom and dad came to see me and stayed with me and I remember I borrowed my Grandmother's seal and mink coat for a prop during a love scene. As I threw it across the stage I heard an audible gasp coming from Mom as she saw her pride and joy being thrown carelessly on the stage.

The thing is, my grandfather was a furrier and my grandmother always visited Sundays wearing that coat and later my mother only wore it on special occasions.

My next parts were at the Theatre in Action in the West Village which was still the Meat Packing District.

I remember walking to the theatre with the stench

of meat butchering in the air. The studio where we rehearsed was actually in an abandoned meat packing plant.

The director of Theatre in Action was Lev Schectman, who was a Russian director from the Moscow Art Theatre. He was a sweet man and I learned a lot from him.

My first part in Theatre in Action was as Marla in the play, *The Misunderstanding*, a drama about a relationship gone awry. You could say it was a preview of what was to come in the reality of my life.

I also played in two classic parts there. One as Anya in *The Cherry Orchard* by Anton Chekov (a Russian playwright) and also as Willie in *This Property is Condemned*, a part made famous by Natalie Woods in film.

The thing is, my only way to support myself during this time was waiting tables, because none of these parts paid anything. They were all just part of my training and demonstrated the "Catch 22" of not being able to get paid parts without an agent and not being able to get an agent without parts as credits on your resume.

The only paid acting parts I got while in New York was as an extra on *One Life to Live*, and in the crowd scene running from the imaginary marshmallow man in *Ghostbusters* as we ran down Central Park West. For each of these parts I was paid the scale rate of extras, which was a grand total of $100.

However, in the film, I was first introduced to Kraft Services so you could say I got the added bonus of free meals!

Back when I was trying to break into the Broadway play scene, I worked at Columbus Restaurant, after Amy's Pub and Formerly Joe's. It was located on Columbus and 76th Street, very close to Central Park. One of my regular customers there was Angelica Houston and her then boyfriend Robert who was an artist. A painter, I think.

Anyway, they came in every weekend at the celebrity table, which was table 5A, where she would hang out with the likes of Dennis Hopper, Julia Roberts, Raul Julia and many others. Drew Barrymore was around there too, with her parents, because she was only about 7 back then. She used to follow me around and begged to wait on tables and hold my tray as she followed me around. She got a real kick out of it but did nothing but slow me down.

Kids weren't allowed in the kitchen so after I took an order she would have to go back to her table as I went to the kitchen with the "dupes" (duplicate order sheets) to give the chef.

Bottom line is, time was money back then, and

the more I turned tables the more money I made.

Angelica carried that air of celebrity wherever she went as she meandered from table to table as she met with other celebrities and "A listers."

Of course, Drew's grandfather was John Barrymore, one of the most celebrated actors of his time. And Drew is following in his footsteps these days.

One of the owners, Paul Herman, commonly known as Paulie, was greatly responsible for all the hubbub of celebrities who showed up there, partly due to his schmoozing them. But the restaurant itself was very understated. I never saw a limo pull up there. Celebrities would slip in incognito. It was a place for working dinners, where deals were put together for shows.

The recent and short-lived TV show *Smash*, which Angelica starred in, shows off those behind-the-scenes everyday things that actors and show people do to make ends meet and try to get a successful show on with good reviews.

It was nice to see a show that realistically portrays what happens to the people who may or may not become stars in their chosen profession. And it was nice to see that Angelica can still put in a good performance.

As you can surmise, most of the celebrities I met

in NYC were at restaurants where I worked, not as fellow actors. I also met Mike Grabow, who gave me a great deal on a rent-controlled apartment in the West Village, complete with a courtyard and ivy growing up the bricks. So even if I wasn't making a good living, I was living well. I'm happy to say Mike has stayed in touch with me after all these years and I count him as a friend!

This screen shot of my MTV video jockey audition tape was made by my then boyfriend Brad Tatum and given to Producer Mark Burnett.

Chapter 6

A Major In Watressing & Bartending

We were watching *CBS Sunday Morning* one day and saw Roma Downey and her husband Mark Burnett being interviewed for their very successful series called *The Bible* on the History Channel. Seeing Mark Burnett brought back memories.

After the interview, I turned to Richard and said, "I made an audition tape for Mark after waiting on him at Formerly Joe's Restaurant in the West Village of Manhattan."

This was in the early 1990s and Mark was at that time in production at MTV and I wanted to become an MTV VJ (video jockey).

Richard had previously recorded my original VHS tape recording onto a DVD to make sure it stood the test of time.

I told him I made a reference directly to Mark on the video tape, and sure enough when we played the DVD copy again, what I remembered saying was there, "Mark, you know I'm a good waitress because that's where you found me."

Burnett is best known for his Survival reality series among many others such as *The Voice*, which I love.

I remember that Mark suggested I do a very natural stream-of-conscious video tape audition in my apartment for which my then boyfriend Brad served as cameraman. I jokingly referred to him in the audition as my technician.

It was ironic seeing myself run through my then apartment talking about music, playing my stereo, discussing my upcoming trip to Florida, showing off my bathing suits and talking about my "skin condition" which I hoped would clear up in the Florida sunshine. (These days, although I can't run around any more, my mind is still quick and bouncing all over the place.)

Seeing myself running all around doing things I can't do now due to the MS gives me mixed feelings. The MS will no longer allow me to run around, but it also got me centered and forced me to slow down and change my perspective to enjoy the now instead of always chasing after the future. I enclose a screen shot I had Richard take from the video of me playing my tape deck with some Elton John music on it to show my stuff for Mark and the producers at MTV. (Remember, big hair was "in" back then!) It's nice to see Mark is still successfully producing after all these years and that he seems happy in his marriage to Roma Downey.

When I finally got around to watching the musical "Rent," I found it brought back a lot of memories of my own time in New York City pursuing acting.

I predominantly supported myself by working in restaurants and subsequently living week to week often having a hard time making my own rent. I lived first in Hell's Kitchen, specifically on the corner of 47th Street and 8th Avenue. I remember it was a tenement walk-up and I bartended down the road at a sleezy bar on 8th Avenue called Amy's Pub. It was owned by a very temperamental and impatient Greek man. I can still hear him yelling, "Get behind the bar, get to work and quit socializing!"

Cindy Dutton was my very first friend in New York City who let me live in her apartment and also bartended at Amy's and wound up getting me a job there as well. Cindy's younger sister, Stacey, also lived with us for a short while, and I got to be friends with her as well. In fact, when I left Amy's

Pub, Stacey and I went to work in a natural foods restaurant that was just opening in the East Village. I don't remember the name of the place, although the owner was much younger and nicer. As I said earlier, after many years Stacey went on to become a talent agent for most notably, Bon Jovi. All these years later I still keep up with them on Facebook.

This was about the same time I met my friend Deborah Goodrich, who I still correspond with. She once played Erika Kane's sister named Silver on *All My Children*.

I remember Deborah was involved with a guy named Mitchell who was best friends with Sammy Merendino with whom I became involved and eventually moved to Flushing, Queens. (Sammy used to be a drummer for Chubby Checker, by the way.)

It was a different time!

Rent really brings out all the hardships you go through in trying to become an actor or entertainer as you try to keep up with paying your bills.

It was several years later while working on the Upper West Side at a restaurant called "Columbus" that I met my future landlord Michael Grabow, who was kind enough to rent me an apartment in the West Village that had a long waiting list and a beautiful court yard. I remember the custodian's name there was Abraham, a big muscular black man and I lived there with my best friend from childhood Jacques. This was the nicest place I lived in while in New York City and was really more than I could afford if it hadn't been for the kindness of Michael.

The apartment was over $1,000 per month for a one-bedroom and we put a fold-out couch in the living room for Jacques to use. I slept on a four-poster, wooden bed.

Sharing a one-bedroom apartment to save on rent was one of the things in *Rent* that reminded me once again of my time in New York City in the 1980s.

Every Tuesday morning, Jacque would get a trade magazine and we would both walk to a newsstand on Hudson Street to buy the theatrical newspaper called Backstage. They would list open call auditions commonly known as "cattle calls."

Our "pie-in-the-sky" hope was to get an agent and avoid the open calls. That's where contacts like my friend Deborah, who had an agent, came into play. She would recommend me for a meeting after she showed her agent my picture and resume and the rest was up to me. So I would prepare a monologue in anticipation that they would want to see me audition.

And much like the musical *Rent,* there was no storybook ending and it went nowhere.

One particular restaurant that stands out is

Columbus Restaurant on Columbus Avenue and 76th Street in Manhattan's Upper West Side where I worked as a waitress in the 1980s.

There were a lot of silent partners in the restaurant along with primary owners, actor Paulie Herman and well-known ballet dancer Mikhail Baryshnikov.

When I watched the Oscar winning *Silver Linings Playbook*, I was delighted to see Paulie in an early scene playing Robert DeNiro's best buddy, Randy.

Although found as Paul Herman on various websites, I knew he and his brother, who both worked at the restaurant as Paulie and Charlie.

Charlie was the antithesis of Paulie personality-wise. Charlie didn't want any of us waiters to socialize with the many actors and well-known personalities who came to the restaurant. He didn't even want us to socialize with any of the regulars there.

For Charlie, it was more important to "turn the tables" quickly with his regulars so that more customers could be served and the restaurant could make more money.

This was the same restaurant where Mike Tyson had the audacity to leave a $2 tip for a $100 bottle of Dom Perignon champagne at which time I had to pull him aside and say, "Mike, this is not cool where normal tipping is 20 percent, especially when you can afford it," as most of the patrons could and would do. He didn't know what "20 percent" of $100 was, so I told him and held out my hand; at which point he whipped out a twenty and slapped it in my hand.

He apologized and said he had been raised in a poor, black neighborhood, so he had no experience with buying a $100 bottle of champagne or in how to tip properly.

As I said before, one of the best tips I ever got was from one of the other regulars at Columbus, Mike Grabow, who offered me a rent controlled apartment in the West Greenwich Village on Barrow Street which had a courtyard and ivy-lined brickwork, French windows and a fountain in the center. The MTV video I spoke of was filmed there.   But back to Paulie Herman. He has appeared in many movies such as *Goodfellas, Crazy Heart* and TV series such as *The Sopranos* and *Entourage*.

I remember Paulie as one of the best bosses an aspiring actor could have because he understood having a calling and needing to go out on auditions with a flexible schedule. He would go out of his way with flexibility in hours for aspiring actors by hiring non-aspiring actors who could fill hours while we actors were off on auditions. But non-acting waiters were few and far between in those days.

Some of the other well-known actors I used to see at Columbus included Michael Keaton, Angelica

Houston, Robert DeNiro, well-known film Director Martin Scorsese and this was where Drew Barrymore used to follow me around when she was a child saying she wanted to be a waitress like me when she grew up!

I ruefully responded, "No, you don't!"

I saw Kevin Spacey on a late night show talking about his Netflix series called *House of Cards*, based on a British series of the same name.

Kevin plays Frank Underwood, the House majority whip who has aspirations of becoming Secretary of State, but when that dream isn't realized, he goes on the offensive to get the power and influence peddling in Washinton, D.C. to go his way.

Although I don't know anything about what goes on in Washington, I do know Kevin personally and it was a delight to see him back in a role that he can play so masterfully. As with most celebrities I met at Columbus Restaurant in New York City when I worked there in the late 1980s, he was congenial and personable towards staff and well acquainted with the owners of the restaurant on Columbus Ave.

I liked Kevin a lot and I enjoyed talking with him, and not just about the business.

He was straight about the business of being in the business. He said I should not take the eventual agents and producers I would encounter too seriously, but weigh whatever they said with a grain of salt.

His words were actually more colorful. I'll leave it to your imagination.

When I watched an episode of Charlie Sheen's sitcom *Anger Management*, I found myself laughing out loud at the ingenious jokes and Charlie's near-perfect timing.

In the episode I watched, his father Martin Sheen guest stars as his character's father who fakes symptoms of Alzheimer's disease in order to escape angry women who we find out he has been two-timing.

In watching the father and son Sheens, I fondly remembered waiting on a much younger version of them both back when I was waitressing in New York City and California. I would see them both together and separately but don't recall ever seeing Emilio Estevez, Charlie's brother, with them. They knew the owners of Columbus Restaurant in New York, Charlie and Paulie Herman, who made a fuss over them and seated them at what we referred to as the "star table" which was number 5A.

I also recall waiting on them a couple of years later at the West Beach Cafe in Venice Beach, California. What was nice was they recognized me from previous times back east and it was nice seeing familiar faces 3,000 miles away when everything else was so new to me. It was great to see friendly faces at my new job. It was convenient for me there as well, because I lived on the same street as the restaurant, which was Venice Boulevard and I lived at 403A, one of three guest houses at 403 that my then boyfriend and I rented.

I liked the Sheens and they seemed to return the feeling since they always requested me when they came there to eat. They also brought a great sense of humor. I remember Charlie and I would make jokes and laugh together. When I told them I moved there to become an actress, they said they recalled me waiting on them in New York. I also asked Charlie who his agent was, because I thought he might be amenable to talking to me about that and he was.

I especially remember that the owners at Columbus in New York didn't want the waiters to socialize with the stars, rather they wanted us to be subservient. Things were less formal in California and so I was able to speak more freely with customers at West Beach Cafe.

Meeting the Sheens was a real treat and something I will cherish. It was great to see father and son working together again.

I caught a screening of the original limited series from USA TV called *Political Animals*.

Some people may dispute the adjective "original"

in that Sigourney Weaver's character appears to mirror the real-life path of Hillary Clinton.

And who would have guessed they would see Weaver in a TV series, let alone on cable.

But the star of *Avatar*, *Ghostbusters* and the "Aliens" franchise has stated she loved the role and neither tries to imitate Clinton nor has she ever met her. (As I write this, Hillary is stumping for a presidential nomination, and I won't know the outcome of that until after you read this.)

I guess you could say I had a fleeting association with Weaver when I worked as an extra in the original *Ghostbusters,* but since I was lost in the crowd racing down Central Park West in New York City from the imaginary giant "Stay Puff" man, that association is mostly in my own memory, not on film.

However, Weaver was also a regular at Columbus Restaurant, when I worked there waiting tables at Columbus Avenue and 69th Street in the city, so I have spoken to her and found her to be engaging, funny and kind, unlike the character she plays on *Political Animals.*

This photo by Richard Nilsen shows me with the matchbox my friend Mike Grabow sent from the former Columbus Restaurant that used to give them out as advertising when I worked there.

Chapter 7

Memories of Restaurants That Were

My dear friend Michael Grabow sent me a memento that really brought back memories.

After he emailed me telling me he had a special surprise for me from the restaurant where I met him, he said a friend from those days had something that would take me back in time - which in fact it did.

I worked at Columbus Restaurant located at 201 Columbus Avenue and 69th Street which was just a block away from Central Park West back in the 1980s. It was also a couple blocks from Lincoln Center.

The reason this is significant is because back then you could still smoke in restaurants.

I met Michael and his then wife Joann while waiting on them. They were regulars that came week after week. Joanne has sadly passed away.

Now keep in mind this restaurant was a celebrity

hang out. Michael and his wife were rare at the restaurant because they were not famous like so many of the other customers were.

This is where I met many celebrities as I was waiting on them. Drew Barrymore and her family were some of the first people I waited on. Drew was just a young child back then and she got a real kick out of following me around "helping" me waitress. I remember she said she'd like to be a waitress someday. Right.

I also met Angelica Huston, who was also very nice and had a very throaty laugh.

So Mike sent me a matchbox that was used as advertising as well as a convenience for the smokers of the day. All it has on it is a picture of a yellow street sign that has the writing "Columbus." On one side of the matchbox it has the address and phone number of the restaurant and on the other side it has a spot to strike the match. This was long before the computer age so there is no website on it.

The matchbox design is typical of the vibe Columbus gave off. There is no hype about what great drinks or meals were served there, just the name, address and phone number. If you were interested you would find out more for yourself or you just got the message through word of mouth.

I remember Kevin Spacey and his entourage

were regulars there and sat at table 5A, which was the celebrity table. They were always kind and good tippers.

The restaurant was owned by Paul and Charlie Hermann. Paul had appeared as an extra in movies and his brother Charlie was more the business man of the two. Charlie wasn't as nice as Paul, often yelling at the wait staff in front of customers. Yikes.

But overall, Columbus brings back great memories of the many celebrities I met there and great customers like Mike Grabow, who I especially want to thank for sending me this remembrance of my past history waitressing as I pursued my acting dreams.

While I was watching *Late Night with Jimmy Fallon* on a Friday night, Fallon was interviewing Christian Slater about a new series he was in called "Breaking In."

Back then I was particularly drawn to the Friday night shows because I found Fallon's "Thank You Notes" segments especially hilarious. Since he has taken over the Tonight Show, I miss those segments.

As I was watching Christian Slater being interviewed, I was reminded of his mother, Mary Jo Slater, who was a casting director. I knew her from my days in New York City.

She would often come to Columbus which was

a well-known spot for being a celebrity hangout. I also wound up waiting on show people such as Julia Roberts, Dennis Hopper and Gerard Depardieu.

It was one night when Mary Jo was sitting with Gerard and Sigourney Weaver going very intently over a script together that I walked up and asked, "Hey, guys, what's going on? Can I grab your drinks from the bar?"

It was at that moment I realized what they were looking at and I quipped, "Drinks are on me if I can get an audition for whatever you are going over."

Everyone laughed, probably both at my boldness and easy going manner with these well-known show people.

Mary Jo kindly gave me her card and said I could call her to arrange for a reading.

The movie script they were going over was the comedy "One Woman or Two," which came out in 1985. So I guess that helps date me and my time in New York City.

Well, I did read for a part before Mary Jo Slater and was actually a featured extra in the movie, although the film itself wasn't a particular success.

As a featured extra, you might get highlighted in a scene even though you don't have any lines and won't show up in the credits.

Still, the scene would be staged as such so that

a featured extra would be close to the stars and therefore be noticeable rather than lost in a crowd scene as I was in *Ghostbusters*.

Although I was just a passerby as an extra in that movie, I did strike up a professional relationship with Mary Jo and she tried to help me get other parts in movies and TV.

Right now I can't think of any special successes she had with me, but her efforts were much appreciated and I still have those fond memories.

I never knew who I might get to wait on back in those days, usually no one that would become well-known. But that particular night made an impression on me and I thought once again of Mary Jo's kindness as I saw her son Christian on Jimmy Fallon.

Growing up, my mother would take me to Howard Johnson's because you got a free cake and ice cream on your birthday. My mother called me every year on my birthday, no matter where I was. As I got older I graduated to nicer restaurants and celebrated with fellow waiters and bartenders I worked with.

I remember I used to go every year when I worked at Columbus Restaurant in New York City to a bar next door I incorrectly remember as "The Emerald Isle." We'd pile in there after hours and the bartender, who was also the owner, was really nice to us.

I got a correction from my old friend Raj Bahadur:

"You mean 'The Emerald Inn' around 69th and Columbus? I used to go there a lot during my 17 years on Central Park West. I remember running into Philip Seymour Hoffman on occasion. When I wasn't there on a Friday night, I'd be at O'Hurley's on 72nd between Broadway and Columbus. Anyway, bad news. The Emerald Inn closed as did O'Hurley's. All the shops around there are really getting gouged for rent. You wouldn't even recognize the neighborhood."

When I was bartending and waitressing, about 70 percent of my pay came from tips as compared to hourly wage. Back in the day I was only paid about $2.50 per hour.

Two seemingly unrelated, recent articles brought this to my attention.

First, I read about Mike Tyson and his hobby racing pigeons. What drew me to the article was a picture of Mike holding a pigeon at an event about racing pigeons. I admit to know nothing about the subject, but I do remember waiting on Mike back in New York City at Columbus Restaurant on Columbus Avenue and 69th Street.

The second article was about Gov. Cuomo's proposed minimum wage hike for hospitality workers to $7.50 from the current $4.90 rate. The lower rate is predicated on the idea that most of tipped workers get their pay from tips and not hourly wage. But that isn't always true. My encounter with Mike Tyson is a case in point. It went as follows.

Mike was sitting at my station which was one of seven tables I was responsible for. He was on a date drinking a $100 bottle of champagne, no food or appetizers, just nursing the bottle slowly and basically holding court for his admirers while I was losing money and patience.

The owners of the restaurant, Charlie and Paulie Herman, cared more about the clientele than the wait staff, so Mike's clogging up a table was my problem, not theirs.

When Mike finally got up to leave, he left a $2 tip for his $100 tab. I was furious. I grabbed the $2 and said, "Look, Mike. This isn't right. This is how I make my living, with tips. You sat at my table for a good two turns. You're allowed to stay as long as you want, but I have to pay bills."

To give Mike his due, he apologized, said he wasn't raised around money and didn't really know the right amount to tip. He asked what I thought would be fair. I said $20 and held out my hand. Without missing a beat, he reached in his pocket and took out a twenty. He handed me the twenty and said, "This is all new to me." You could say it was a teaching moment. He was back at my table weekly and never made the same mistake again. In fact, he requested my station thereafter. I think that the experience growing up tough made him respect the confrontation.

There were times when I got a great tip however. That same night, I got a wonderful tip from property owner Mike Grabow who offered me a rent controlled apartment with an open court yard in the West Village that I snapped up and wound up being very happy living there.

But some customers weren't so easy to work with.

I remember a French family of tourists who came to my station at Chumley's and had a multi-course dinner and then left 22 cents for a tip.

I was so irritated I chased them out of the restaurant up onto Bedford Street and threw the coins after them. I can't print what I said to them. I was hot.

Thereafter, my mantra was, "Tipping is not a city in China." In fact, according to a New York Post article, one bar threatened to have the phrase printed on T-shirts for the wait staff. It is often found on tip jars and near the register at check out.

*　　*　　*　　*　　*

One day I was watching *CBS Sunday* and saw one of the featured stories was about actor Danny Aiello. Back in the 1980s when I was working at Columbus

Restaurant in New York City I met Danny who was a regular there and good friends with owner Paulie Herman. I became very close to Danny, so much so I used to call him "Uncle Danny."

When he was working on Broadway in a play I remember him calling me from backstage when I was in my West Village apartment.

He was calling just to talk between scenes. I remember he was talking in a very hushed tone so as not to interrupt whoever was going onstage.

He was excited to be in a Broadway play, to kill time between scenes and just to talk. I was a confidant sharing his thoughts about the play, *The House of Blue Leaves* and his role in it.

I learned some new things about him during the segment on *CBS Sunday*.

For instance, that he worked as a baggage man for Greyhound Bus because he needed a steadier income after getting married to Sandy Cohen.

Up to then he had been a shoe shine boy, in the army during the Korean War where he entertained the troops as a baseball player and then became a pool hustler.

I knew about his history as a shoe shine boy, his military service and pool player but not about his working for Greyhound.

He also said he was desperate enough to be a safe

cracker for awhile, which was news to me.

He said he backed into acting at age 36 after a stint as MC at a comedy improv club, where he realized he was a natural entertainer.

He has since been in 90 movies as well as several Broadway plays. He even got an Oscar nomination for his part in *Do the Right Thing*.

His response to not winning the Academy Award was typical of his outlook. "Who me? Danny Aiello win an award for acting? I never studied a day!"

Yet his first role in *Bang the Drum Slowly* was opposite Robert DeNiro, who he quipped never could play baseball even though Danny tried to help him learn the game.

It appears Danny gave lessons on ball playing while DeNiro exchanged with some tips on acting during the film.

Danny was always very kind, generous, outgoing and always thought of himself last, putting everyone else before him. You don't see too many actors with that outlook in the business. I will always think of him fondly.

At the time I didn't realize what a great voice he had. He has released some albums of big band music and he has a great Tony Bennett sounding voice.

I researched his albums on the Web and listened to some cuts from his albums and I immediately ordered one.

Thing is, instead of showing concern or boasting about his own career, he was concerned about me and my career, such as it was.

I remember he told me to "Look out for the vultures. They'll eat you up." Good advice in any career.

Kathryn J. Spira

This head shot shows me with shoulder-length hair and was most likely taken in the late 1980s when I was still in New York City.

Chapter 8

More Restaurants & Celebrities

Training Drew Barrymore to be a waitress

Back when I was working at Columbus Restaurant in New York City, Drew Barrymore used to come in with her parents when she was about 7 years old. This was about the time of her break-out acting part as Gertie, the younger sister of Elliot in *E.T.* in 1982.

Her parents John Drew Barrymore and Ildiko' Jaid Barrymore were friends with the owners of Columbus.

The owners pretty much fawned over the Barrymores, since they were such a well known acting family. (John's father, John Sidney Blyth Barrymore, has been called the greatest actor of his generation.)

I was waiting on their table and Drew was fascinated with what I was doing. She thought it was magical that I was bringing food and she could eat it.

She asked, "Please, could I be a waitress with you someday?"

At the time I was dreading her following me around because I had a lot of tables to wait on and she would slow me down. She was adorable and chatty, but that didn't go with my busy job.

I told her she could stay with me for about ten minutes and then I had to go back to the kitchen where she was not allowed. The chef would have gone nuts.

We went from table to table. The front area was all celebrities and they were all ooing and aahing over Drew, being the youngest of the Barrymore acting dynasty.

She was too small to handle the dishes, and she couldn't reach the tables, so I couldn't actually have her "help" me serve, so I sent her back to her parents table where they could deal with her.

While they were eating, other patrons didn't bother them, but when they were done, other celebrities would stop by to talk.

Drew was precocious, dressed adorably and seemed to handle herself well around all the fray. She wasn't a screamer and really loved the attention. At least I didn't see any acting out while I was "training her" to be a waitress.

A couple of years later, her parents divorced and

I know she was in rehab at an early age. Once out of rehab, I believe she has stayed out and established her own production company with the "Charlie's Angels" movies as a couple of her successes.

Truth to be told, it would be very unlikely that Drew would ever have to be a waitress in real life. Her course was set for her from an early age.

Forbidden Foods at Formerly Joe's

Back when I was living in New York City and working in the West Village in Manhattan I used to work at a place called Formerly Joe's.

It was on the corner of West Fourth and 10th Street and the tongue-in-cheek name referred to the former "Joe's Place."

They did lunch and dinner with a raw bar and a fully stocked regular bar.

This is the restaurant I worked with Edie Falco (waitress), Anthony Bourdain (oyster and clam shucker behind the raw bar) and Michael Chiklis (waiter).

Every afternoon before the dinner rush, we would sit down at the designated staff table and eat whatever the owner and chef came up with-usually leftovers from the night before. But because the owner was a bit of a cheapskate, certain foods were off limits.

One such item I always tried to scarf was linguini

with white clam sauce. Michael liked spaghetti with meatballs, so he was easy to please.

Edie liked raw food that was strictly off limits because of the cost.

The chef also made a great chocolate fudge cake that was off-limits. We all liked it and stole to eat whenever we had the opportunity.

I remember one way we got the cake was by writing extra dupes for it. The dupes were receipts for orders that would have to appear on the bill.

We just hoped the owner wouldn't check the extra dupes against the register tapes.

Unfortunately Andy Menschel, the owner, knew all the tricks, since he used to be a waiter himself. So we rarely got away with it.

He made us pay for the cake or off-limits food items we took.

I remember hiding in the kitchen with Edie and Michael, gobbling down fudge cake and giggling like children during slow times. The problem was, the chef, a Chinese guy named Pahn, was in cahoots with the owner to try to catch us at it. So we not only had to rectify things with Andy but also with the kitchen staff.

It was Menschel who gave Chiklis a hard time when Mike was offered the role of John Belushi in the feature film *Wired*. Chiklis wound up leaving the job for the film opportunity and from there his career took off.

After Chiklis left (owing me money he had borrowed for his Con Ed electric bill), Edie and I continued to work there for some time. We both left about the same time; she heading out to Hollywood and me going to another restaurant in the city called Columbus Restaurant on the Upper West Side which I've spoken about before.

Since their humble beginnings, both Chick and Falco went on to win Emmys for their respective roles-his in *The Shield*, and Edie, of course, in *The Sopranos*. I have to tell you, I've never seen *The Sopranos*, and what little I saw of *The Shield* was too gritty for me.

But I will always remember the times we had laughing and eating together in the kitchen and staff table at Formerly Joe's.

*   *   *   *   *

In New York City I used to go to what we called "Tar Beach," which was on the rooftops of apartment buildings. My best friend and former roommate Jacques and my girlfriends would gather to tan on our personal beach on the rooftop.

It was very hot up there, so hot I would wind up

taking the Long Island Railroad out to Jones Beach when I craved the real sand and water.

My friend Edie Falco, who later won Emmys for her portrayal in *The Sopranos* and now has starred in *Nurse Jackie* for several seasons would sometimes accompany me to both "Tar Beach" and "Jones Beach" before we went to work at "Formerly Joe's" restaurant and bar in the West Village of Manhattan. Edie was just a regular person and good friend back then when we were both trying to break into acting.

I remember when Edie won her first Emmy for her role in *The Sopranos* she was interviewed by David Letterman on his show.

He asked her to tell some stories about acting and she said she didn't have any.

"This is my first job acting," she said. "I only have waitressing stories."

Edie is that kind of down-to-earth person. Never any airs.

After our times at either beach, we would hurry back home to shower and change for work at the restaurant which usually started between 4 p.m. and 6 p.m. and ended about 2 a.m.

Afterwards we would go to after-hours bars and then off to breakfast at a 24-hour diner or a Denny's.

Sometimes, when I wanted to spend more time at the beach, especially at Jones Beach, I'd take my uniform with me and put it on over my bathing suit. I actually did that more often than hurrying home for a shower because it would take away from my beach time.

So during the summer you could say I'm always in uniform!

My friend Mary Woltz was hostess at Formerly Joe's, and with her southern charm, it was a wonderful way to greet the patrons. She was hostess there when I was a waitress.

(This was also where we worked with Michael Chiklis, Anthony Bourdain and Edie Falco.

They have all gone on to be quite successful, while Mary and I have gone other routes.)

Mary is a southern gal and loves the country. She raises bees out Montauk Point, Long Island these days, although the last we visited her, she had an apartment in the Upper East Side near the East River.

She also visited us up here in the Adirondacks one year and we had a great time cross country skiing at Lapland Lake.

At the time I met Mary, I had only lived in cities, but we hit it off right away.

I remember she was with us when we were hiding from the owner, Andy Menschell (*not* a nice guy but fair) at "Formerly Joe's" in the kitchen along with Anthony, Edie and Michael as we scarfed down the chef's chocolate mousse cake when we were supposed to be working at our wait stations.

Ah, memories!

According to a New York Times article, Joe's closed in 1992 due to a lease dispute between Andy and the building's owner, Joe's widow.

Mary and I are both now in our 50s and lead very different lives from our days in the Big Apple.

As a side note, I saw Edie Falco on a talk show one night as her *Nurse Jackie* series was about to start it's sixth season (worth watching, by the way).

Anyway, when asked by, (I think it was Seth Myers) about acting stories, she said she had many more waitressing stories as she'd "worked in every restaurant in New York City, most of which are no longer in business."

I know that's true of Formerly Joe's as well as many other places I worked at in the city.

Edie mentioned she would have nightmares about forgetting something at a table or drink orders, and I have to say I've had those nightmares too.

Mary had a natural bent towards hospitality and would make people very comfortable and in a good mood to order the specials as well as drinks — very important in the restaurant business.

She always tried to give me a full station of tables and made my work there very pleasant.

Owner in the House

It's a rare thing today to speak directly to the person in charge. One that comes to mind from my acting days is Paul Herman.

I knew Paul as "Paulie" Herman.

In the 1980s, Herman dated Bernadette Peters. He was a co-owner of Columbus Cafe along with ballet great Mikhail Baryshnikov. It was located on Columbus Avenue near Lincoln Center.

I was a waitress and sometimes bartender at Columbus.

Paulie always answered the phone at the restaurant when he was there and always personally greeted patrons, especially the many actors and notables who frequented the place like Kevin Spacey, Julia Roberts, Angelica Huston, Danny Aiello and Michael Keaton just to name a few.

According to Wikipedia:

"In 2009's Crazy Heart, Herman played the tough, successful agent/manager Jack Greene to Jeff Bridges' rough, drunk Oscar-award-winning singer."

Herman has also made appearances in movies such as *Once Upon a Time in America*, *Silver Linings Playbook*, *Analyze That*, and *American Hustle.* He also had a recurring role on *The Sopranos* as "Beansie" Gaeta, as well as another HBO series, *Entourage*, as Vincent Chase's accountant, Marvin.

Unfortunately, Paulie's brother Charlie was the one who usually dealt with the wait staff. Charlie was a miserable person to deal with.

I remember Paulie asking me to nicely show then 7-year-old Drew Barrymore how to waitress as she kept begging me saying she wanted to be a waitress just like me! Hah!

Brother Charlie told me not to be friendly to the customers, just to wait on them, which was in direct conflict with what Paulie had said and how I am. In contrast Paulie was always going from table to table talking to the patrons, often sitting and chatting.

I remember my friend, patron Mike Grabow, coming to my defense and telling Charlie not to treat me like that. (Mike gave me a great tip by offering one of his rent-controlled apartments in the West Village which even had a court yard as I said earlier.)

I'm shivering with Mary Woltz by the East River in NYC
November 2000. Mary was hostess at Formerly Joe's when I
worked with her and Edie Falco, Michael Chikliss and Anthony Bourdain. The photo was taken by Richard Nilsen.

These Peter Max sketches of me were done over 20 years apart. The latest was done from memory when my Mom saw Peter at an art show of his work in Cleveland in 2006 and the earlier one was done in 1986 when I was waiting tables in NYC and he asked me to stop moving a moment so he could sketch me.

Chapter 9

My Time in the Big Apple

The artist Peter Max was someone I knew when I was working in New York City, so much so that he took me up to his art studio and I witnessed his art first hand.

He also sketched my profile when I was working at a restaurant where he frequented and in 2006 when he visited Cleveland with an art show, my mother asked him if he remembered me, and he said not only did he remember me, but he immediately sketched me from memory.

I have the original sketch from 1986 and the one from 20 years later in 2006 together on my wall above my computer.

Max is best know for his pop art posters of the Beatles and the movie *Yellow Submarine* (although the production team of the film denied that Max had anything to do with the movie), but he's painted many presidents and other celebrities as well as being the official artist for Super Bowls of the past.

I got thinking about New York City due to the effect of Hurricane Sandy. Not that I was glued to the TV for details, but I did happen to tune in to CNN and ABC TV coverage of the storm which was pretty complete at the time.

I was shocked to see people walking waist-high in flood waters and to hear that 46 miles of the subway was flooded.

Back when I was pursuing an acting career in NYC I walked most places but if I had to go any distances I took the subway. Taxis were inefficient in that they took longer than the subway as well as being a luxury.

As I write this to you, I remember the No. 7 train that used to take me out to Flushing New York where I lived with a boyfriend named Sammy for awhile. After Flushing I lived in midtown Manhattan, the Upper East Side, then, finally, in the heart of Greenwich Village at 72 Barrow Street which was on the corner with Hudson Street.

I never saw any shutdowns of any part of the transit system while I was living there.

I remember when I lived on West 91st and 2nd Avenue, I would take the No. 2 train 70 blocks south to the West Village where I worked at a bar/restaurant called Formerly Joe's on the corner of West Fourth and 10th Street. From that restaurant I had to take a taxi home because although the subways ran all night, it wasn't safe for me to travel alone at those hours.

I found it heartbreaking that such a glorious city was under water. From the pictures I viewed on the news it appeared a daunting task.

In general, I agreed with the comments made about New Yorkers taking everything in stride and not letting this storm get them down.

I happened to see the Late Night with Jimmy Fallon Show on the night of the storm and both he and fellow host Dave Letterman felt it wasn't safe for audiences to be present, but they each went on with their shows in spite of having no audience.

That's the spirit of "the show must go on" I remember from my days in the Big Apple, and it was good to see they still felt that way.

A Winter Sweater and
Remembering Michael Keaton

The winter of 2014-15 was especially cold in the northeast. The reason I bring this up is because when I wore my warmest sweater one day I remembered that I got it at a store called the Banana Republic in New York City about 35 years ago.

Banana Republic was in the Soho area of lower Manhattan. Soho stands for South of Houston Street "pronounced Howstin."

It was here that I met the actor Michael Keaton. The reason I bring up the sweater is because I bought it right after meeting him. That in of itself is a funny story.

I was walking into Banana Republic and he was walking out at the same time. I'm like "Oh my God, Michael Keaton! I love you!" Without missing a beat he quickly replied asking me what my name was.

Flustered but very excited I said "Kathryn Spira," to which he answered immediately, "Oh my God, Kathryn Spira! I love you, too!" I was so thrilled that I said very rapidly, "No I mean your movies but I love you anyway. I am an actress and I really think you are a great actor."

He kind of looked bemused and amused at the same time saying, "Well, good luck to you as an actress." He hailed a taxi and I went into the store speechless.

It was while in the store that I bought this very cool hunter green and off white snowflake sweater which was knit on both sides. It is because I wore this sweater one day in an especially cold spell that I retold the story.

I remember he starred in a movie called "Mr. Mom" back in the 1980s. This is the type of movie I always imagined myself being in as an actress. Though I have no personal knowledge of the whole concept of parenting, I think because of my disinterest and ignorance about parenting I found the movie hilarious as Keaton found himself struggling with parenting issues.

I remember Terry Garr's character chiding her

husband because he had no idea about the difficulties of day-to-day parenting. (Terry is another actress who had to deal with MS.)

There was a scene when he was in a grocery store with his kids and they were pulling everything off of the shelves that they could reach. He was having a hard time saying no and keeping control. Though he was not sure of what foods to get, he was sure sugary foods were not the way to go.

A particularly hilarious scene showed Keaton trying to describe his grocery store experience to his wife and she just rolled her eyes and said, "You don't have to explain this to me. I did it a lot longer than you."

Through the course of the film, Keaton finds new found respect for his wife and the work she did child rearing during all of the years he worked outside of the home. The conclusion of the film brings normalcy back to Keaton's life, but I'm not going to ruin it for you in case you haven't seen it.

I'll keep my sweater and my personal memories of Michael Keaton alive with my sweater as a reminder.

When I moved to New York City to pursue acting, I adopted Jones Beach as my summer activity area. I would ride the Long Island Railroad out to the beach as often as I could so long as it didn't interfere with my waitressing job.

Memories of Tar Beach

Wherever I lived when I was in New York City pursuing my acting career, when I couldn't make the two-hour trip back and forth to the beaches in the Hamptons on the Long Island Railroad, I would head to tar beach.

Tar beach was a colloquialism for those of us who loved the sun so much that we went to the roof tops to "lay out."

Now, you talk about baking with not so much as a breath of fresh air, and forget about luxury, ocean-side sunbathing. I would lay out on a foldable recliner on the asphalt coated with tar of the flat roofs of the apartment house I was living in at the time.

Most memorable of those tar beaches, was 72 Barrow Street in the heart of the West Village of Manhattan.

I talked about this apartment building before and how much I loved living there. What a coup it was getting this apartment because I was waiting on the owner of the building, Mike Grabow and his wife, at Columbus Restaurant.

I always wanted to look healthy and glowing for any auditions I went to while trying to get acting jobs. I never wore makeup, so a healthy glow was obtained from the sun. This was before warnings about skin cancer and using sun block became so prevalent. In fact, I used baby oil to magnify the sun's potency, as opposed to my current practice of coating my skin with SPF50 Ocean Potion for the ultimate in skin protection.

It was a classic brick building flowing with ivy with a courtyard and every apartment was resplendent with casement windows and tall ceilings.

Waiting on Mike week after week eventually brought up the question about where I lived. When I answered "Hell's Kitchen," he said that's got to be rough.

He reached in his pocket and gave me a card explaining about the building he owned and told me there was a vacancy.

I was all over this idea, phoned him the following morning and we met at apartment 2D where I signed a lease and gave him a deposit. It was about $1,000 per month which I split with my roommate Jacques. It was only a one-bedroom but Jacques had a fold-out, futon couch which doubled as a bed at night.

Vacation Time for Actors Too

I'm going to fast-forward to my time in Hollywood, although a lot of this applies to my time in New York City too.

Since pilot season for new TV shows in Hollywood generally runs from January to early March, by summertime, if I wasn't involved in an actual production or summer stock plays, I, along with other actors, was on vacation.

This is one area where the crazy schedule for acting is more similar to normal work schedules. But I didn't really see this time as vacation time so much as time to take a break from my efforts to realize my acting dream.

Summer was also a time to devote to bar tending and working on my tan at the beach so I would look my best for any auditions or head shots made later in the year.

I didn't just lay in the sun at the beach. I took the opportunity to exercise by running, since one of the assets I listed on my acting resume was being athletic as well as a runner.

I would run on the beach and then take a dip in the ocean and I would make sure to wear my bathing suit instead of underwear to work in summer, a habit I still maintain today even though I no longer can run.

Summer was also a time when I could visit Mom and Dad or they could come out to N.Y.C. or L.A. and I wouldn't be as busy chasing my dream with auditions and readings.

Acting classes were held year round, but I often took summers off as the instructors liked to take their own vacation breaks during the summer months.

When I was in New York City during the summer, it was so hot that I often took the Long Island Railroad out to the Hamptons to see my eldest sister, Linda, who lived there with her family. Sadly she is now deceased having lost her battle with breast cancer several years ago.

Summers in L.A. were hot, but there was no humidity to speak of in comparison with N.Y.C., so it never seemed as oppressive.

By the end of summer, with my tan and runner/swimming body in shape, I was at my best and made sure to get my head shots and other photos ready for the coming season of auditions.

So far this summer, we've had great weather and my tan is looking good. However, on the down side, we were seriously lacking rain in the spring for vegetable gardens and flowers, something I never worried about when I was chasing my acting dream. How things change with time!

My best friend growing up, Jacques Lorenzo, filled a blank book with sketches and humorous notes about my life. Here is what he wrote about my going to the beach. It's in three parts beginning here and continuing on page 93 and 103.

Chapter 10

My Friend Jacques & His Book of Me

One of my favorite presents of all time was a book my wonderful friend Jacques made about my life.

Jacques sadly passed away in 1995, but we were very close at one time and he knew me well.

Jacques surprised me with a beautiful hard-bound book of blank pages (like you might have for a fancy journal) which he filled with illustrations and a narrative about my life up to that time. He wrote about me with truth and humor using several running gags about my being boy-crazy, loving the beach and so on.

I miss him so much... even looking through this book brings me close to tears. He knew that I was both boy-crazy and the boys liked me too.

At the age 28 he followed me to New York City so we could both try to become famous as actors.

For months we would practice our acceptance speeches for the Oscars. His day job (until we were 'rich and famous') was working at a shoe store called "To Boot" in the lower West Village. My day job, which was really mostly at night, was as a waitress at a restaurant called "Formerly Joe's" on West 4th and West 10th Street just steps from where we lived at 72 Barrow Street.

We had known each other since drama classes for the youth theater at Wiley Junior High School in University Heights, Ohio not far from where I grew up. We were doing kids' plays there. It was run by a guy named Mr. Leonard.

Jacques came all the way from Solon for the weekend classes. I was never actually in a production there, but Jacques was and we formed a bond for many years. He was my first experience with a gay boy and told me "all I needed to know" about that at the time.

"You know how you like boys?" he said. "Well I do too, and that's all you need to know about being gay."

Because of the way he presented it, I never thought being gay was a big deal, and I still don't.

Jacques knew me so well, probably better than I knew myself at the time. He knew I would drop everything for a boy, even if it was foolish to do so. He knew that I could find peace at the beach and that's how I am now to this day. I'm just a lot more calm when it comes to boys, since Richard and I have been together 20 years now.

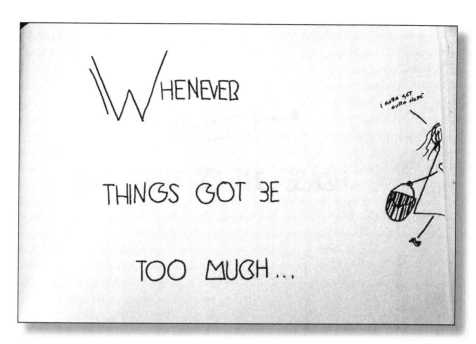

I enclose illustrations from the book including my "happy place" at the beach as well as a photo of me. (I now live on a lake with a private beach, so I'm always in my happy place.)

I have wonderful loving memories of my friend Jacques and the book that Jacques had written about me. It is written like a children's book, because there are very few words and colorful, hand-drawn pictures. He starts the book by simply writing "Once there was a girl, by a friend," that was page one.

Now you have to understand this is actually a sketch book with a hard binder and its size is 11 inches wide x 8 1/2 inches. The next page says copyrighted 1988 in his same cartoon print. I'm not going to go page by page with you guys because it would take way too long.

I knew Jacques since we were both 12 and we shared many experiences as well as personal secrets. I think it was when we were fifteen that he said to me about his being gay.

The recent passage of gay marriage rights throughout the country makes me think how differently Jacques might think about his love of New York City, which is where he lived for years.

Some of the great things about having a gay friend for an apartment–mate is that he kept things neat, festively decorated and kind of made for a built-in shield from unwanted male suitors (who he was sure weren't good for me.)

I think the thing that was a sore point in our relationship is when I chose to move to California with my then boyfriend, Brad, who he didn't like and didn't think would be good for me. Turns out he was right.

But that's a different story. The book he made for me was a labor of love and chronicles my boy-chasing ways as well as the boys who chased back. Ultimately, he knew I would find peace somewhere at the beach and made that clear in the last line of the book. I enclose a sample to show how dear his creation was to me.

Working as an Extra
I recently heard a new movie was being filmed in

Albany and there was a call for extras. (I think it was called "Beyond the Pines.") This is the second such call that I've heard of being sent out in Albany. The first was for an Angelina Jolie film, *Salt*.

As an aspiring actress, I started out as an extra on *One Life to Live*, a soap opera. This was when I was living in New York City. I was just starting my career and hoping it would take off from there.

I remember going to the newsstand every Wednesday as early as possible to get a copy of Backstage, which had a listing of auditions, predominantly "cattle calls" for extras.

It was very difficult getting a talent agent as an unknown. Basically, when I made a query call, I was asked what my credits were. The Catch-22 was, you couldn't get an agent without credits, and you couldn't get credits without an agent.

So I concentrated on off-off Broadway shows whose audition listings were also in Backstage. Hundreds of people showed up for the parts with the same idea I had-to build up credits on the resume.

I remember I put everything I had ever done in high school, my time with the American Repertory Theater Company (called ART Reach) and my modeling jobs in Cleveland so I could fill up a resume sheet. I also added all the community theater I did in Cleveland.

What comes to mind as I write this is working for the

Chagrin Valley Little Theater in Chagrin Falls, a suburb of Cleveland. This was where I met my dear friend Jacques. I can't think of the place without thinking of him. Before he sadly passed away he also was an aspiring actor in New York City. As I said before, while I worked in restaurants as a waitress, Jacques worked in a high-end shoe store called To Boot.

Jacques was never a fan of working as an extra. He hoped to move directly to feature work. Subsequently he became a great shoe salesman.

I tried to go the more conventional route of putting a head shot and resume together and send it to all the agents listed in the Ross Reports, another weekly booklet listing all the New York talent agents with their mailing address but never their phone numbers, because they didn't want to get phone calls during the day from wannabe actors.

I hoped my work as an extra would lead to being picked out by a casting director for a speaking role which would eventually lead to feature roles.

Since extra roles only gave you work for one day at a time, even though they paid $50 to $100 a day and meals, I didn't always go for the extra roles because I didn't want to be known as a "professional extra" by a potential agent.

There was always the elusive hope of being plucked out of the extra ranks by a director, but that was unlikely, since there were hundreds of us in each movie production. I had about as much chance as you have to pick me out of the crowd in *Ghostbusters* or *The Doors*.

Watching 'Rent' Brings Back Memories

I finally got around to watching the musical *Rent*, and found it brought back a lot of memories of my own time in New York City pursuing acting.

I predominantly supported myself by working in restaurants and subsequently living week to week often having a hard time making my own rent.

I lived first in Hell's Kitchen, specifically on the corner of 47th Street and 8th Avenue. I remember it was a tenement walk-up and I bartended down the road at a sleezy bar on 8th Avenue called Amy's Pub.

It was owned by a very temperamental and impatient Greek man. I can still hear him yelling, "Get behind the bar, get to work and quit socializing!"

Cindy Dutton was my very first friend in New York City who let me live in her apartment and also bartended at Amy's and wound up getting me a job there as well. Cindy's younger sister, Stacey, also lived with us for a short while, and I got to be friends with her as well.

In fact, when I left Amy's Pub, Stacey and I went to work in a natural foods restaurant that was just opening in the East Village. I don't remember the name of the place, although the owner was much younger and nicer.

I believe after many years Stacey went on to become a talent agent for most notably, Bon Jovi.

All these years later I still keep up with them on Facebook.

This was about the same time I met my friend Deborah Goodrich, who I still correspond with. She once played Erika Kane's sister named Silver on *All My Children*.

I remember Deborah was involved with a guy named Mitchell who was best friends with Sammy Merendino with whom I became involved and eventually moved to Flushing, Queens. (Sammy used to be a drummer for Chubby Checker, by the way.)

It was a different time!

Rent really brings out all the hardships you go through in trying to become an actor or entertainer as you try to keep up with paying your bills.

It was several years later while working on the Upper West Side at a restaurant called "Columbus" that I met my future landlord Michael Grabow, who was kind enough to rent me an apartment in the West Village that had a long waiting list and a beautiful court yard. I remember the custodian's name there was Abraham, a big muscular black man and I lived there with my best friend from childhood Jacques. This was the nicest place I lived in while in New York City and was really more than I could afford if it hadn't been for the kindness of Michael.

The apartment was over $1,000 per month for a one-bedroom and we put a fold-out couch in the living room for Jacques to use. I slept on a four-poster, wooden bed.

Sharing a one-bedroom apartment to save on rent was one of the things in "Rent" that reminded me once again of my time in New York City in the 1980s.

Every Tuesday morning, Jacque would get a trade magazine and we would both walk to a newsstand on Hudson Street to buy the theatrical newspaper called Backstage. They would list open call auditions commonly known as "cattle calls."

Our "pie-in-the-sky" hope was to get an agent and avoid the open calls. That's where contacts like my friend Deborah, who had an agent, came into play. She would recommend me for a meeting after she showed her agent my picture and resume and the rest was up to me. So I would prepare a monologue in anticipation that they would want to see me audition.

And much like the musical "Rent," there was no storybook ending and it went nowhere.

Celebrating New Year's Eve

New Year's Eve was always a big celebration when I was growing up in Cleveland. My Mom would always have a party complete with a bartender so she didn't have to worry about mixing drinks and could be part of the social celebration.

My adopted father, Joe, had a portable bar he would bring up from the basement so the bartender could tend bar with all the alcohol behind the bar so it would look like a cocktail party, not just a house party. She liked things just so like that. The bartender wore a tuxedo and guests wore dresses and suits. Things seemed to be a lot more formal back then.

I should interject here that my Mom and biological Dad divorced when I was about five, so I was raised mostly by Joe, who I called Dad all his life. In recent years I have become reconciled with Arnie, my biological father, and I think I have a pretty good relationship with him and my "step-mom" Reggie. I hope they feel the same.

Anyway, Mom would have appetizers rather than a full meal served and about 20 or 30 people would attend including both family and friends.

Mom had five siblings and I remember her oldest brother, Uncle Erry and she would exchange New Year's gifts rather than Christmas gifts because they were Jewish.

One gift in particular went back and forth between their homes. It was a "Shalom!" sign that they considered particularly tacky, and the thing was, whoever was visiting would leave the sign hidden somewhere in the other person's home to find later and have a good laugh.

Being raised Jewish, Thanksgiving and New Year's Eve were celebrated instead of Christmas and I didn't miss it because it had never been a part of our tradition.

Another part of the New Year's tradition was a game of charades which always evoked much laughter.

I remember Mom would get tipsy at New Year's Eve parties and would sometimes feel sick later, which should have served as a cautionary tale for me, but didn't have that effect. (Later, when working as a bartender, I remember we used to call it "amateur night" because of the people who would get drunk without realizing how sick it might leave them. And of course these days, the dangers of drinking and driving have come to the fore.)

After leaving home, I continued the New Year's Eve tradition with my best friend Jacques when we both lived in New York City as far as watching the ball drop but with much smaller groups of friends in. Sometimes I had to work bartending New Year's Eve which was good in that it was a big money night and all the bartenders fought to get the shift.

My holiday traditions involved my mom and sisters driving around out of our neighborhood seeing all the Christmas lights since, being Jewish, we didn't have our own decorations and neither did our Jewish neighbors.

I was introduced to putting up a Christmas tree and decorations through my best friend, Jacques, when I lived in New York City. We used to decorate with red velvet bows and white lace bows on the tree which we dragged up from the Christmas tree lot by the Hudson River in the West Village. We also got a string of tiny white lights to garnish the tree without any colored lights or other ornaments.

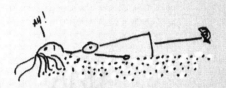

SHE WENT TO THE BEACH.

I can hardly be recognized with "big hair" and holding a tray in this screenshot from *The Doors* directed by Oliver Stone and shot on location at the Whisky A Go Go in Los Angeles.

Chapter 11

A New Fiancé & Off to Hollyweird

On Moving and Getting an Agent

It was in the late 1980s I left New York City with then boyfriend Brad who was cast in a pilot for the TV show *Mulberry Street*.

So off to California we went. I specifically remember renting a big U-Haul truck loading up all of our stuff, including two cats, and taking to the open road. It was a long and arduous trip, not to mention uncomfortable as the truck bounced us around.

It was probably not a great idea traveling with the cats in the cab. I had the brilliant idea to fill up a cardboard box with litter so they could do their business. Well you know what they say about the best laid plans....the cats never used the box.

While watching Brad shoot the pilot, the man I sat next to was a theatrical agent named Tom Jennings. We struck up a conversation about myself as a struggling actress and Brad an actor who had just moved from the east coast to the West.

To make a long story short, I had an appointment with Tom the next day in his Beverly Hills office. I showed up with my head shots and resume. We searched to find the best photo to represent me and a game plan to launch me. He wanted me to meet "the right people."

As it turns out he never really had a very well thought-out plan for my career. Tom remained my agent for all the time I lived in LA. But he was busier drinking than working...which made me a very successful waitress.

He did get me a "featured extra" role in the 1991 movie *The Doors*, starring Val Kilmer and Meg Ryan. I got to play a waitress (how ironic!) at the Whisky A Go Go in Los Angeles on Sunset Boulevard which was shot on location.

I remember the shoot was very dark with Oliver Stone setting the mood for Val's character Jim Morrison to go gradually nuts on stage.

(By the way, this particular scene is definitely *not* G-rated.)

It's about 35 minutes into the film and I can be seen on the right holding a tray of drinks, but I'm not very recognizable.

Oh, well, that's show business!

The shoot did take two or three nights, so even at scale, I did make a little money.

Unfortunately it didn't lead to anything bigger.

I should say here that I refer to Brad these days as "bankruptcy Brad" rather ruefully. See, we moved out to California for his big break at a series opposite Connie Sellecca called *Mulberry Street* that never made it past shooting of a pilot. We first rented 403-A North Venice Bouevard then bought a house near the ocean at 634 Crestmore Place also in Venice Beach that we couldn't afford and wound up having to give it back to the bank. Ah, youth.

It was actually when I left Brad for another guy that in retaliation he saddled me with the entire house mortgage payment that had been originally worked out due to his trust fund. I had no such fund but with my name on the mortgage, I struggled with bartending to make the payments each month. I was forced to file bankruptcy.

I remember the judge asking me how a young lady like myself could get that far into debt. I simply answered, "an angry ex-boyfriend," and that's when I named him "Bankruptcy Brad" and Chapter 7 went through thus messing up my credit for years thereafter.

But back to my career hopes. Many pilots are shot in hopes of being "picked up" by a network studio, but fail to do so for a variety of reasons. They may lack backers or sponsors or just not be the "flavor of the season" that year.

According to Suite101, "Pilot season is when shows in development are given the go-ahead and casting begins. Traditionally, January is considered the beginning of pilot season, though some begin casting as early as November. In May, the networks present their new shows to advertisers in New York, typically flying in their celebrities to help excite the advertisers about buying airtime."

What pilot season meant to me and the thousands of unemployed actors in California was the hope that we would audition for and be "discovered" as fresh talent. However, what I found was that in order to get an audition for a new show, you had to have credits and a resume ready-made, which was a Catch-22 for a new actor just starting out. This is where it became crucial that you have a pushy agent that really believed in you.

The agent I spoke of earlier, Tom Jennings, I met while at the filming of the pilot for *Mulberry Street*, when I was there in support of Brad. There were many talent agents in the studio audience perusing the cast for fresh talent and I happened to be sitting a few seats away from Tom who was looking for new talent. In fact I think he was there hoping to sign Joely

Fisher, who was in the cast with Brad. Fisher is the daughter of singer Eddie Fisher and actress Connie Stevens. Her half sister is actress Carrie Fisher, who is most famous for her portrayal of Princess Leia in the original Star Wars trilogy.

I have to say both Connie Sellecca and Fisher were very nice to Brad and me, as were the rest of the cast and crew. And by the time of the wrap party for the pilot, I was having drinks with Tom, had his business card and an appointment for the following week.

He became my agent for years after that while I lived in California and I had high hopes. I know he had some long-time soap opera stars on his roster that were his bread and butter. But my high hopes never really bore any fruit.

Extra Work

There was a trade paper back then called Backstage which in the back part listed upcoming extra work.

I remember pouring through the paper looking for extra work. I got my first job as an extra in the movie *Ghostbusters* while I was still living in New York City.

There were 100s of us extras running down Central Park West as part of the scene being chased by the ghost "Stay Puft" marshmallow man. We were paid at the then-rate of about $100 per day and that scene only provided one day's work.

But I did get to put *Ghostbusters* on my theatrical resumé, just as I later got to put *The Doors* on my resumé out in L.A. The difference being I was "featured" as a waitress in the scene where the Doors were singing at the Whiskey A Go-Go.

Since most of my actual paying work at the time was as a waitress or bartender, playing a waitress in *The Doors* was ironic. I guess you could say I had plenty of experience.

One of the difficulties about being an extra was how difficult it could be to look natural just walking, running or making "conversation" as an extra.

One regular extra *CBS Sunday* interviewed said she would silently mouth "peas and carrots, peas and carrots" to other extras to look natural. The next level of acting work was called "under five work" which was a step above that of an extra because you had five or less words spoken in a scene.

I got to say my "under five" in the soap, *One Life to Live* while I was still back in NYC. That got me my AFTRA card (American Federation of Television and Radio Artists) so I could, presumably, get more TV work. That was my plan anyway.

Bottom line is, those were my humble beginnings in the movie business. And as they showed on CBS

Sunday, that's where actors like Jack Nicholson and Brad Pitt got started too.

So as they say, "Hey, you never know."

Remembering a 'Table Read'

In watching an episode of *Curb Your Enthusiasm* about a Seinfeld Show reunion, creator and director Larry David stages a show within a show by having a "table read," which has the cast sit down at a table and read the script in character as it was written.

It was fun to watch characters George, Elaine, Newman, Kramer and of course Jerry Seinfeld reprising their former roles. Adding to the fun is the conflicts within the group as they are preparing to do the table read.

For every play I've ever done, we had a table read with the full cast which wasn't as much fun as in the *Curb Your Enthusiasm* show, but did give the cast their first chance to sit down together and get to know each other in character.

In *One Woman or Two*, I remember my character and my then boyfriend Brad character were in conflict with another couple and our parents due to the strained living conditions with each other.

In the story, both couples were living with their parents as newlyweds while trying to find their own homes.

The director would give us tips on how to relate to one another in the scenes. I remember my character was alienating her parents because they disapproved of my new groom.

The irony here was that Brad and I were actually engaged at the time and there was no harmony between my parents and him either. My efforts to win my parents over eventually ended when I realized they were right, and he was indeed a deadbeat. Oh, well.

The *Curb Your Enthusiasm* episode I watched not only brought back memories of the table reads I used to do for plays I was in back when I was an aspiring actress, it also brought back how much I enjoyed the characters and show. It was great fun watching them play themselves with all their foibles.

Springtime for Actors in L.A.

Springtime for actors out west in Los Angeles is very different from what I've been experiencing here in upstate New York.

In the spring in California it was pretty consistent with the temperature between 70 and 80, dry and sunny. Only the month of February brought rain and cooler temperatures, say in the 50s, but rarely freezing like I see here. But the sunny weather did cause me to miss the four seasons' changes which I enjoy here.

Any of the houses I lived in when I was in California had small sources of heat, because it just wasn't needed very often. Central air conditioning was much more common and needed more often than heat.

Actors would start auditioning for fall TV pilot's in late February and early March. We called it "pilot season" in the industry and actors like myself and our agents were feverishly trying to land parts so we would have parts to film in the summer and early fall.

For instance, it was in the spring that I was cast to play the part of Daisy Mae in a Monday Night Movie of the Week based on *The Beverly Hillbillies* television series that never made it to production due to lack of funding and proper planning by the production company. That was also my fate in the planned TV series *Sibs*, which never made it into production.

I got "sides" of scripts to read, which consisted of about 12 pages of dialogue, but never saw the whole script for either production. As opposed to my fledgling efforts, my then fiancé Brad would be sent full scripts, because he had credits in full productions and his Screen Actor's Guild (SAG) card and a great agent who would go to bat for him. I remember he tried to get me an audition with his agent, but because I had no TV credits, his agent wouldn't see me.

That was the catch-22. You couldn't get an agent without TV credits and you couldn't get TV credits without an agent.

It was rare that an unknown would get a meaty roll.

It took a combination of persistence, talent, knowing the right people and luck.

My Last California Apartment

It was 323 N. Spaulding Ave. in West Hollywood where I spent my last days as an aspiring actress in California.

I tended bar at the West Beach Café where I met fellow bartender Dana, who I asked to tend bar at Brad's and my wedding. Problem is, I totally fell for Dana, which leads me to my next place of residence in Beachwood Canyon, Hollywood with my now boyfriend Dana, who was also an aspiring actor.

Dana and I shared war stories of both auditions and bartending experiences and we seemed to have a lot in common. But alas, Dana broke my heart and my girlfriend Geri Miller introduced me to another dear friend Michael Bruno, who was at the time looking for a roommate. Michael was a great roommate because he was both gay and a theatrical agent. He worked for the prestigious agency International Creative Management, known in the industry as simply ICM.

It wasn't my intent to try to manipulate Michael, but I did hope he could move my career forward with proper representation because ICM was known for taking on new and young talent.

But since you needed credits to get an agent and you needed an agent to get auditions which would hopefully lead to acting credits, Michael wasn't really able to help me unless I was first able to help myself.

When I was working at a West Hollywood eatery called A Votre Sante ("To Your Health," in French), my MS rose to the fore and was particularly difficult to get to the bar, which was upstairs a total of 38 steps on an outdoors entrance to the bar.

It was there while working a wrap party for *The Flintstones* movie that John Goodman graciously helped me stock the bar when he saw my difficulties and advised me to leave Hollywood, "There are sharks out there," he said, and that whatever was going on in my body was more important than seeking acting credits.

So that made Spaulding Avenue my last stop out of Dodge, as they say, and eventually led me to my current view of a beautiful Adirondack lake and beach.

Learning About Stars on Biography Channel

I was watching a show about Morgan Freeman and his beginnings as an actor from the Biography cable channel.

This was a new channel for me, and scrolled through the variety of stars covered on the channel and was intrigued to find that my old pal Julia Roberts was listed.

So I obviously tuned into that one next. I already knew she had been raised in Smyrna, Georgia and that her first film role was in the independently produced *Mystic Pizza*. That was about the time I knew her in New York and later caught up with her in California at a birthday party for a mutual friend.

It was during this time in New York when she was engaged to Jason Patrick and I was engaged to Brad, as I said earlier, but it wasn't until years later in L.A. when she was with Kieffer Sutherland and I was with Dana that we ruefully laughed about our bad choices in men back then.

The biography channel touched on each relationship Julia had, noting one of the strangest was her marriage to country singer Lyle Lovett, though in simple terms, Julia simply loved him. This and other relationships she had came after we had lost touch.

I also watched the biography of James Dean, the

quirky actor who died in a sports car accident, and learned he was always taking chances, both in his art and his relationships. What surprised me was that he was bi-sexual in a time that really didn't accept that and I had never heard that before. He was accepted into the prestigious Actor's Studio, but quit when a film part in *East of Eden* came his way, where he was nearly cast opposite Paul Newman, who interestingly didn't make it into the film.

The point being, I've learned a lot of little known facts about stars before they became stars.

Any experiences I had with stars came through waiting on them in restaurants and bars or working with them before they got their big breaks, as I have previously told you guys about with Edie Falco, Michael Chikliss and Anthony Bourdain. In contrast, I knew Julia through a mutual friend.

Going to a Birthday Party with Julia

When I was living in Los Angeles my dear friend Deborah Goodrich had a birthday party at a restaurant on Ocean Avenue between Santa Monica and Malibu. It sat across the street facing the ocean. Hence the name of the street.

I had been friends with Julia Roberts since my days in New York City. And Deborah had befriended her as Julia's then boyfriend had been a line producer on a feature film Deborah was in.

I had also met Deborah in New York City. I met her at a restaurant in 57th Street because my then boyfriend Sammy was friends with her then boyfriend Mitchell. Our friendship survived the loss of both boyfriends.

Deborah used to play Silver Kane, sister of Erika Kane on *All My Children*. What's ironic about that is that I was a die-hard *All My* fan for years.

Anyway, I think it was Deborah's 30th birthday and she arranged for all of her friends to meet at this restaurant, and for once I wasn't working.

About 12 or 15 of us got together, all girls, and it was just a coincidence I had known both Julia and Deborah before the party.

I had been to Deborah's house in some canyon around L.A., I forget which one. I think at the time, Julia was living with Kiefer Sutherland in the Hollywood Hills. Anyway, she didn't bring Kiefer with her because it was an all female party.

I'm trying to think of what man was in my life at that time. As far as I can remember, it was Bradford Tatum.

We all had seafood at the party as well as birthday cake and cocktails.

I remember having mimosas which is champagne, orange juice and triple sec or cointreau, which is like a fine orange liqueur.

Everybody at the birthday party were "in the business" in some form or other. Deborah's agent and Julia's publicist were both there, I remember as well as a couple of female directors. These were all people Deborah had personal or professional relationships with.

Deborah now lives in Connecticut with her family and is no longer part of that profession. But I'm glad I still keep in touch with her at least via e-mail and Christmas cards. I've often wished I could contact Julia again, but I lost touch with her as her career took off and she has buffers between her and the general public. Deborah told me she no longer stays in touch with Julia either.

KATHRYN SPIRA

This photos of me squatting in cut-off denims and the Look magazine cover of Daria Halprin (on page 123), whose resemblance to me was one of the reasons my friend Raj Bahadur thought Dennis Hopper took a shine to me.

Chapter 12

West Coast Restaurants & Dennis Hopper

While I was in California there was a contest between bartenders for "the best margarita."

At the time I was working at the Kachina Grill in downtown L.A. The margarita contest was promoted by the makers of Patron Tequila and the bars and restaurants of L.A. County who served that brand.

Since Kachina Grill catered to Mexican food and drink lovers, it was a natural for the winning cocktail drink mix.

There are plenty of cocktail mixes I used to know by heart and have forgotten over the years.

And there are even more that have been introduced since I served my last drink.

Movies like *Cocktail* starring Tom Cruise illustrated how fast bartenders were encouraged to pump out drinks to make the restaurant profitable. I never used a shot glass since I knew how much to pour out by eye and feel and because it would have slowed down serving drinks.

I remember my fellow bartenders and friends Dana, Rick and I used to race each other at the West Beach Cafe in making lemon drops, a favorite drink there at the beach. When we had time after hours, we would sample the various drinks we made routinely to fine tune the mixes and make them better.

By the way, to make a Bay Breeze, a shot of Grey Goose vodka, and equal parts of Ocean Spray cranberry cocktail and Dole pineapple juice is about right.

Pour the three over ice and mix.

You can increase the cranberry juice for more tartness or increase the pineapple for added sweetness.

Anyway, my Margarita was chosen as the winner that year and the mix went something like this: two shots of Patron Silver Tequila, about one and a third shot of Cointreau liqueur, about a shot and a half of fresh-squeezed lime juice all poured over a two-thirds full glass shaker of crushed ice and shaken with an aluminum cup fitted over the top and then shaken together.

The Kachina Grill was also where I was written up in a Southwest dining magazine by two food critics who used to hang with me Saturday nights where it tended to

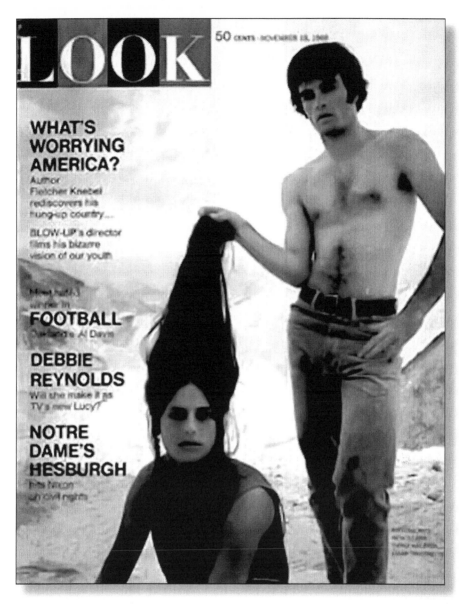

be pretty quiet because it was in the financial district and weekends were slow there compared to after office hours on Monday through Friday.

It was the West Coast version of Wall Street clientele.

When they did a write-up of the restaurant, they said the food was okay but the "hilarious bartender named Kathryn" (actually they spelled my name wrong and that always bugged me) kept us entertained. Well, as I said before, as an actor I was a very successful waitress and bartender!

Another place I worked at was A Votre Sante ("to your health"). The owner there wasn't very nice but his wife, actress Tia Carrerra was very nice to the staff and made the job more enjoyable.

I still have a "Hugo Boss" denim shirt the owner gave me when I worked there.

Actually Tia made him give it to me when I admired it. She definitely wore the pants in that relationship!

And then of course there was my time at West Beach Café with Dennis Hopper, Anjelica Huston and the Sheen boys, Charlie and his father Martin. Once again the owner was difficult, not wanting us to hob nob with the celebrities, but since I knew several of them from my East Coast waitress work, I wound up being pretty friendly with them anyway.

Shirts Bring Back Memories

Getting a shirt from an owner has been a bit of a theme with me and quite a few shirts along the way.

As I was putting on my Hollywood Athletic Club sweatshirt one day, it got me thinking about the various restaurants and bars I worked in while pursuing my acting career.

The shirt was typical in that it was off someone else's back, in this case my old friend Dana, who worked at the Hollywood Athletic Club at the time. I like it so much that when the sleeve cuffs started to fray, I had them repaired so I could keep wearing it.

The Hollywood Athletic Club really was an athletic club long before it became a bar-restaurant. According to Wikipedia:

"The building at 6525 Sunset Blvd. was built in 1926 by Meyer & Holler, the same architectural firm that built the Grauman's Chinese Theatre and the Egyptian Theatre.

At the time it was the tallest building in Hollywood. During its early years as a health club, its membership included Johnny Weissmuller, Errol Flynn, Charlie Chaplin, John Wayne, Walt Disney, John Ford, Douglas Fairbanks Sr, Mary Pickford, Cecile B. de Mille, Cornel Wildle, Humphrey Bogart, Clark Gable, Jean Harlow, Frances X Bushman, Howard Hughes, Joan Crawford. and Rudolph Valentino."

Keeping with tradition, the staff were all aspiring actors and entertainment people. It wasn't by design, but unemployed actors tended to gravitate towards the restaurant and bar business as I did.

Other shirts I have connected to bars and restaurants include my Dark Socks T-shirt which was connected to the West Beach Café, where I worked along with other mostly unemployed entertainment hopefuls. The shirt was for a softball team started by 12 of the restaurant staff but not actually sponsored by the restaurant. The owners weren't really very supportive of the team. As far as the owners saw it, actors just made for scheduling problems while trying to further their careers with acting gigs and auditions.

When the shirt wore out, while it was still recognizable I had a local T-shirt company reproduce it for me with "Spira" personalized on both white and gray backgrounds for summer wear. I also got to return the favor to Dana by sending him and his new bride personalized Dark Socks T-shirts as wedding presents.

I also have a Reel Inn T-shirt from a restaurant-bar in L.A. The original shirt was given to me by the owner of the fresh fish place along the Pacific Coast Highway in California in Malibu.

According to a review of the restaurant, "the original PCH outpost is right across from Topanga State Beach--the witty sign scribbled with dishes such as "Oh My Cod" is definitely eye-catching. The patio overlooks the highway, but visiting neighborhood cats add a certain charm. The food: Fresh seafood from around the globe is the reason to head to this glorified seaside shack.

When the shirt wore out, I asked my friend Dana to replace it and he did, with a newer version which I still wear today.

My Sinatra Tapes as a Tip

I've just been listening to some tapes I've had for a very long time. They are actually studio recordings of Frank Sinatra that I received as a tip back in 1990. What is specifically written on each cassette tape, (I have just three) is "Test Recording from Specialty Records Corporation, Analog, Account: Warner Bros, Sel #: 4-26340 Tape 1,2,3, Artist: Frank Sinatra" and nothing under the title designation.

Not being a Sinatra fan, but familiar with his commonly recorded music, I must tell you that neither I nor Herman recognized much of the music he was singing on the tapes. In trying to rethink where and when I received these tapes though, I kept thinking it was New York, but Herman quickly reminded me that I was in California by 1990. And of course, that's where Warner Brothers Studios is located.

It isn't that I don't like that style of music. In fact, I am a huge fan of Michael Feinstein who collects swing music of the 1930s and beyond. You may have seen a documentary of his collecting and performances on PBS recently called, *American Songbook.*

Of course, Feinstein is more of my era than Sinatra, and I have in fact seen him in concert when I was in Sarasota, Florida visiting Mom one winter when she was on vacation.

According to the PBS special, Feinstein still carries on a hectic concert schedule, with as many as 500 concerts in any one year. The fact that he makes time to search out and collect songs and tapes and videos of period music that might otherwise be destroyed says a lot about his love of big band, swing, jazz and Broadway music of the period.

But back to these Sinatra tapes; Herman and I played them on our stereo and they were such clear studio recordings that they didn't really seem like cassettes at all. I would never part with these recordings, however, in researching some studio recordings of Sinatra's on line I learned that they could be quite expensive for the right collector.

My Time with the Original 'Easy Rider'

I was watching the news one day in 2010 and I learned that Dennis Hopper finally succumbed to prostate cancer and died.

At the time, I was so upset that I immediately had to turn away from the television to write down my thoughts in honor of Dennis.

I watched his iconic 1969 classic *Easy Rider* in memory of his life and death, although it took me two sessions.

Although it's not really my kind of movie, I certainly

can understand what it represents for that day and as a counterculture movie of an era. It was a time of both doing and dealing drugs for both America and apparently Dennis as well. In Dennis's words in an interview with *CBS Sunday* back in 2008, he was drinking a half-gallon of rum and 18 beers a day along with snorting 3 grams of cocaine "just to maintain" at one point. But he said he'd been clean and sober the last 24 years.

I knew him as a regular guy at the restaurant where I worked, the West Beach Café on Venice Boulevard in Venice Beach where he lived until the day he died.

Dennis was one of the regular guys who on more than one occasion "had my back" with the owners of the restaurant and stood up for me. He ate often at the bar, liked Eggs Benedict and often started his Sunday morning in those days with a mimosa.

He would switch back and forth between the bar and a table as I specifically remember at the celebrity table "5A," a big round table in the corner of the restaurant.

He was never one to show off with fanfare or bravado. He just kind of slunk in on his own and later he would join his friends at the celebrity table.

I just knew him as Dennis, my bar buddy, who would have a laugh over a margarita.

I'm told he was in more than 100 movies during his career in spite of an eight-year hiatus after a difficult time with the director of *From Hell to Texas* in 1958. He later said, that director Henry Hathaway told him when he came back to movies in *The Sons of Katy Elder* he wasn't a better actor, just smarter.

But we didn't talk that much about movies. His focus was on life in the now.

He would ask me how I was doing and I'd start to talk about my difficulties with my agent and auditions.

He'd say, "No, no, Kathryn. That's not what I'm talking about. I don't mean the 'business.' I mean, what makes you happy?"

Because he talked business with everyone in his life. But with me he focused on what mattered the most.

Then when I said, "Going out that door on the beach with the wind and surf and sun," and he'd say, "I'm right there with you, Kathryn."

He said that's why he still lived in Venice Beach.

And that's where he died.

He was one of those who was looking out for my well being, and warned me, "This town is full of sharks."

I have nothing but fond memories of my time with Dennis.

Afternoons with Dennis Hopper

Before he died, I have to admit I had mixed feelings when I heard the news that Dennis Hopper had finally been given a star on the Hollywood Walk of Fame.

I was delighted on his behalf when they showed him

on camera smiling at the cheering crowd as he accepted the accolades of so many fans, but was saddened at how frail he looked.

He was putting on a brave face for the crowd, but the news that he had cancer of the prostate and looked so sickly was truly upsetting to me.

When I knew Dennis in Los Angeles, he was a regular at the West Beach Café in Venice Beach and used to spend the entire afternoon parked first at the bar with me and my crew and then withdrew with friends to a table to have dinner.

I knew Dennis as one of the good guys because he treated me as an equal.

It may have been because of his background, coming off a farm in Kansas to Hollywood.

I remember seeing *Rebel Without A Cause*, where Hopper appeared with James Dean in the 1955 classic. And of the more than 100 films Dennis has been in, he may be best remembered for writing, directing and starring in the classic *Easy Rider* with Peter Fonda.

Dennis used to really like my margaritas, so much so that I even shared my recipe with him.

I went as far as to show him how to mix and serve the drink with the top-shelf ingredients I used.

Where he and I parted company, was that he always liked the rim of his margarita glass salted and I don't.

He was so down to earth and always curious about the

world around him.

Like John Goodman, Dennis warned me about the "sharks" in Hollywood.

The owners of the West Beach Café, Rebecca and Bruce Marder, took themselves way too seriously, and Dennis recognized this in them and was an open ear to my frustrations about them. He stood up for me more than once when I had a conflict with them.

I read that Jack Nicholson, Viggo Mortensen, Dwight Yoakum and director David Lynch were on hand to help honor Dennis when he got his star. Dennis was valiantly looking beyond his current health problems when he received the honor, and this is something I can identify with in my own life.

Suffice it to say, Dennis Hopper was one of the good guys in Hollywood.

Dennis Hopper and the Grasshopper Martini

The West Beach Café was a convenient walk to work from where I lived then.

There wasn't really a booming breakfast business, although they had a great weekend brunch. On the weekends I worked the brunch and week days I worked lunches to mid-afternoon.

The real brass ring was getting the night shift. That's where the most money was to be made.

However, I did pretty good on weekend brunches,

making $100 to $150 per shift.

Dennis was one of the semi-regulars at the café. He both ate and drank there. When he came for a regular meal he would sit at a table, but when he ate brunch there he often sat at the bar.

He was irreverent in nature, as you might expect, and didn't really understand all the fuss made over him by the owners and patrons alike. I found him to be pretty down to earth.

Some of my favorite memories were of putting jazz on the restaurant stereo system located behind the bar and having Dennis help me pick out who to put on that day. I remember he liked Pat Matheny, but don't recall his other likes.

This was before the days of CDs and we had cassette tapes stacked up next to the stereo.

We talked about the business of entertainment, what the heck I was doing out there as a young woman in the rat race. Mainly we discussed not so much the acting business as likes and dislikes about people we knew. He had a strong aversion to people falling over themselves to try to get an audience with him as if he was some kind of a guru.

Thing is, he was in iconic films with James Dean, Peter Fonda and Marlon Brando. At the bar he often sat with Angelica Huston with whom he was good friends. None of this meant a thing to me, I just liked talking to him as a regular guy and he seemed to like that attitude.

My bartending buddy Dana, who worked with me there, remembers Dennis liking a drink called a Grasshopper martini. I can't remember if it was named for Hopper or if it was just a drink he liked.

Suffice it to say, I was not terribly impressed with his reputation, just that he was a bar regular and a great guy to talk to. (And a great tipper and a great friend.)

When I saw him later in TV commercials, where he acted kind of tongue in cheek, it took me back to those days in L.A. when Dennis and I were just talking about nothing in particular.

At the time I wrote about my recollections of Dennis Hopper, there was a mix of opinions about the guy. Seems not everyone saw him as the good guy I knew. He was apparently in the throes of a messy divorce and legal property dispute shortly before his death.

But then, Dennis was complex. Many may not know him as a great photographer and artist.

My old friend Raj emailed me his recollections of Dennis when he interviewed Hopper for a magazine he worked for. He mentioned changes in Hopper's political views as well as why Hopper may have taken a shine to me.

"Those were some great Hopper recollections!" Raj said of my column.

"When I interviewed him (for the movie, *Speed*), he

was deep into his Republican phase, wearing an Armani suit and disavowing everything about *Easy Rider*, including his own character. It was like telling a little kid there's no Santa Claus. As opposed to Peter Fonda, for whom I did my 'bad Dennis Hopper' impersonation from *Easy Rider*, the scene where they're in jail and Hopper's stating his case to the sheriff – 'Do you know who this is, man? That's Captain America! I'm Billy!"

"We're headliners, baby! "

Fonda loved it. At least he pretended he did. The point is, he (Fonda) owns up to the movie to this very day, even if it doesn't always stand the test of time."

A neighbor of ours in Caroga Lake, Bob Fuller, is a long-time Hopper fan and even loaned me a copy of *Easy Rider* after I wrote the column. Bob emailed me the following: "I am saddened by the death of Dennis Hopper, as I know you are. I can't believe he didn't get his star on the Walk of Fame until recently-he deserved it a *long* time ago."

Thanks to Bob for his loan of the movie and comments.

But back to Raj, he thought he knew why Dennis took a shine to me when I used to wait on him in California.

"I don't know if I ever told you this, but the first time I saw you in downtown Cleveland, I thought to myself, 'This girl looks a lot like Daria Halprin.'

Who is Daria Halprin? Daria Halprin was an actress who starred in a cult film from 1970, *Zabriskie Point*.

More importantly, she was Dennis Hopper's third wife and the mother of his daughter, Ruthanna.

I have absolutely no doubt whatsoever that Hopper took one look at you and thought to himself, 'Halprin II!' So that's why he had your back with the owner of that restaurant in Venice! Plus, I'm sure you made a great margarita.

Daria currently teaches "movement" at a place called the Tamalpa Institute in northern California. She and her *Zabriskie Point* co-star, Mark Frechette, made the cover of Look Magazine in 1968. (In real life, he died in prison following a bank robbery.)"

After looking at photos of Daria Halprin, I'm not sure I see the resemblance. (Although I did have the "big hair" Halprin had).

I enclose a photo with the Look cover. You be the judge. I'd much rather think Dennis and I just got along well-or that I made a great margarita-which I did by the way. In a local contest I once won a "best margarita in L.A." award.

KATHRYN SPIRA

In this studio shot I am wearing a plain white T-shirt, a favorite of mine, and what I often wore over a bathing suit when I worked in L.A.

This is me with singer/songwriter Danny Peck at Ghengis Cohen Restaurant in California in 1998. The photo was taken by Richard Nilsen.

Chapter 13

Turning Down a Part (A Poor Career Move) & Photo Ops

Photo Ops Then and Now

Back when I was growing up in Cleveland, Ohio I was in a high school singing group called Girl's Glee Club/Men's Chorus. On a trip to Washington, D.C. I took some photos of my friends at the time, which included one of Sean Young, who later gained fame as an actress who played the love interest role in the Harrison Ford film *Blade Runner*.

Of course, in high school, no one knew who might become a celebrity in later life, so it was just a casual photo of a friend I knew.

As I pursued my own acting career in New York City and then Los Angeles, most of the celebrities I came to know were those I waited on in restaurants. Some, who I worked with in bars and restaurants, were friends as co-workers and later became well-known actors—the exceptions being Danny Aiello (who I used to call "Uncle Danny), Dennis Hopper (who I used to spend Saturday afternoons chatting with at the West Beach Café), artist Peter Max (whose home studio I've visited and who sketched two portraits of me) and Julia Roberts (who I used to double-date with). These were patrons who I waited on and then became friends with.

Others were struggling actors like myself at the time, such as Michael Chikliss (who still owes me money I loaned him to pay his Con-Ed electric bill) and Edie Falco. They've both gone on to win Emmy's in dramatic television series, but at the time they were just co-workers and pals in the restaurant where we worked called "Formerly Joe's," in the West Village. Anthony Bourdain worked there also and I knew him pretty well long before he wrote *Kitchen Confidential* and became a well-known traveling chef. At the time he was a clam and oyster shucker at Joe's raw bar.

I've been asked why I have no photos of myself with them at the time. There are several reasons for that. First of all, who knew who might become famous later? It might have been me!

Also, we were all just co-workers and friends and not trying to cozy up to celebrities or get autographs at the time.

Also, we were young. And when you're young you don't think about looking back on those times with photos or autographs, you think your life will go on like this forever.

I've come to treasure those memories and realize how fleeting time can be. So I've been a bit more apt to have photos taken with those I meet and interview along the way.

I include a couple of photos here, one with singer-songwriter Danny Peck when I saw him in L.A. back in 2000 and another with American Idol Finalist Cara Samantha Aug. 2014 at the Third Annual Caroga Lake Music Festival.

After all, who knows who will become famous in years to come? So I'm getting the photos now!

It was always important in Hollywood to maintain your looks and keep your age private. I never even shared with my agent, Tom Jennings, my true age, always shaving a few years off my age.

People are mystified now when I tell them my age. The general reply is, "I would have guessed 10 years younger."

Years ago I moved around a lot, literally chasing my dream.

In California I ran along the beach to keep in shape and stay fit. I also swam every morning after my run by wearing a bathing suit under my running gear.

Birthdays have always been important to me. I've always been surprised at how some people try to forget their birthdays as they can't face getting older.

That wasn't the case with my family.

Growing up, my mother would take me to Howard Johnson's because you got a free cake and ice cream on your birthday.

My mother called me every year on my birthday, no matter where I was. As I got older I graduated to nicer restaurants and celebrated with fellow waiters and bartenders I worked with.

I remember I used to go every year when I worked at Columbus Restaurant in New York City to a bar next door called "The Emerald Isle."

We'd pile in there after hours and the bartender, who was also the owner, was really nice to us.

Actually, I got a correction from my old friend Raj Bahadur: "You mean the Emerald Inn around 69th and Columbus? I used to go there a lot during my 17 years on Central Park West. I remember running into Philip Seymour Hoffman on occasion.

When I wasn't there on a Friday night, I'd be at O'Hurley's on 72nd between Broadway and Columbus. Anyway, bad news.

The Emerald Inn closed (this was in 2013) As well as O'Hurley's. All the shops around there are really getting gouged for rent. You wouldn't even recognize the neighborhood."

More Memories of Marion the Librarian

It was way back in 1977 at Cleveland Heights High School in Girl's Glee Club/Men's Chorus where I got my first leading role as Marion the Librarian in *The Music Man*.

The subject came up as I was going through old photos and came upon a picture taken of me singing "My White Knight." I remember the director, Bill Thomas, changed the lyrics to "My Bright Knight," so it wouldn't seem to have any racial connotation since our high school was interracial with about half and half black and white student body.

In the picture I am wearing a high-collar, long cotton print dress that came from the wardrobe department, something I never would have had in my closet. I'm sitting on the front porch of my parent's home supposedly dreaming about my co-star Harold Hill (played by Michael Oster, incidentally my first gay leading man who was quite a character). Oster had a beautiful voice which I especially remember from his rendition of the memorable song from the musical "Seventy-six Trombones."

My best friend from high school, Carol Gifford, was in the next musical I was in called *How to Succeed in Business Without Really Trying*, where I played Miss Jones and she played Miss Krump. I remember Carol singing "This Irresistible Paris Original" about a dress and I remember we both laughed so hard we could barely get through the song.

One thing I learned about acting in my first musical was how to seem romantically involved even with a gay man! Also, my character as Marion was very different from my personality.

I remember they wanted me to wear wire-rimmed glasses, which I refused and was the first in a long line of stubborn decisions which probably did my career no good, in that I later refused to appear in a movie scene (*One Woman, Or Two*) with Nick Nolte, which may have advanced my career, but I refused because I would have to appear in the nude and didn't want my first impression on the public to be that. My theatrical agent, Tom Jennings, was really mad at me when I turned it down. I didn't lose him as an agent, but he kind of lost interest in me from that point on.

Revisiting My Favorite Subject

When I was out in southern California chasing my dream of acting in movies and TV, I started wearing men's boxers for both looks and comfort. I confess to borrowing some of my boyfriends' boxers in the same way that I talked guys into letting me borrow their shirts-especially T-shirts with designs I liked. I say borrow with a grain of salt, because I still have some of these items today in my closet.

Of course, I couldn't wear beachwear to auditions. So whenever I went to try out for a part, I had to run home and change to more appropriate clothes that would coordinate with the role I was trying out for. I always kept a change of clothes in my car in case the weather was so magnificent at the beach that I couldn't stand to go home and change. I'd just change in the beach rest room and be on my way into Hollywood for the audition.

One of the parts I tried out for was the character Elaine in Seinfeld's sit-com, which of course was eventually played by Julia Louis-Dreyfus. I was only one of many who tried out for the part, but I hoped for the best because my agent said the actress who would get the part was supposed to have long, curly hair and be funny, which fit my personality and looks.

My agent, Tom Jennings, thought I would be perfect for the part and set up the audition, and in fact when I saw the description of the Elaine character, I thought I would be perfect for it.

Alas, I never even got a call back and the rest, as they say, is history. But I still have my beach and sun time, which always was my priority and still is, so I guess it's not so bad.

Same Dilemma, Different Location

The sun affects me in a very positive way.

As I was recently listening to Cat Stevens "Tea for the Tillerman" while sun bathing, I was reminded how much I tried to do everything while in the sun. But, alas, there are many things that can't be done in the sun, such as I can't write and be in the sun at the same time. Typing, or rather "keyboarding," is of course done on the computer and as everyone knows, the screen is almost impossible to see in the sunlight.

The same problem of feeling drawn to the sun happened in Los Angeles while pursuing my then acting career. Problem being I was and still am mesmerized by the sunshine.

The difference being out there I was on the beach at the ocean. Let me just set the stage. I was living in Venice Beach just a couple of blocks from the beach. I'd get up in the morning put my running gear on, which consisted of boxer shorts, tank, tennis shoes and of course my Walkman radio. I would then walk the two blocks to the beach grabbing a muffin and coffee on the way and hitting the boardwalk to find an empty spot on a bench and eat my breakfast. I would then go to a pay phone which was on the beach and check in with my talent agent Tom Jennings. (This was before cell phones.)

This was always a double edged sword so to speak, because on the one hand I wanted an audition for a TV show or movie, but on the other hand did I want to travel the 45 minutes to the studios in Burbank, where the auditions were held. Jennings knew me pretty well and also knew that my dream of becoming an actress was stronger than being a beach bum.

Let me tell you how this sort of played out. It's really in two parts. Jennings turned out to be not a great agent and my MS was becoming a little more pronounced. I was walking with a fold-up cane back then which I would simply stash in my belt bag and sort of limp into the studio for the audition. Of course this was only the last several years I was out there.

As agents go, Jennings being Irish and a self proclaimed lover of drink evidently became more enthused with that part of his life rather than the talent representative part.

Although I will say he had three major stars that were on daytime soaps, which I believe were his bread and butter.

Agents rarely took on unknown talent like me, so I considered myself lucky in that I had very little theatrical credits on my resume other than my training in New York City and my experience in off-off Broadway shows.

You know, what I ultimately decided back then that remains a constant today is my positive state of mind.

That people are more important than things and that the glory of being an actress really wasn't what I imagined it to be.

In a way my MS has given me the freedom to live the way I want to and really embrace and enjoy every day. Of course the sunny days still shine the brightest for me.

I'm posing with American Idol finalist Cara Samantha in 2014 in Caroga Lake, NY The photo was taken by Richard Nilsen.

This contact sheet of photos shows me and Dana Mosbarger, the bartender I ran off with as a "runaway bride."

Chapter 14

Runaway Bride

You could say I had a real life situation in which I played the part my friend Julia Roberts did in *Runaway Bride*.

I moved from New York City to Los Angeles in the late 1980s with my then boyfriend Brad (who was cast in a pilot for a planned TV series called *Mulberry Street*.)

When Brad and I first moved to L.A., he proposed to me and we lived in a row house at 403 A, Venice Blvd., Venice Beach and I waited tables and tended bar at the West Beach Café which was within walking distance.

At that café I met fellow bartender Dana, who I asked to tend bar at Brad's and my wedding. Problem is, I totally fell for Dana, who was also an aspiring actor.

Working at the West Beach Café together, Dana and I had to hide our relationship from the rest of the staff so we wouldn't be ridiculed and teased. We didn't want to make the relationship public and did all we could to keep it to ourselves.

Since I had been engaged to be married to Brad and actually wound up with the bartender who was to work at the wedding. Well, yeah, you get the picture.

I should add that Dana, who was thought to be a "heartbreaker," actually did eventually break my heart, though we are still friends today. I include a contact sheet of head shots we did together at the beginning of this chapter.

Dana and I shared war stories of both auditions and bartending experiences and we seemed to have a lot in common.

But alas, Dana broke my heart and my girlfriend Geri Miller introduced me to another dear friend Michael Bruno, who was at the time looking for a roommate.

Michael was a great roommate because he was both gay and a theatrical agent. He worked for the prestigious agency International Creative Management, known in the industry as simply ICM.

It wasn't my intent to try to manipulate Michael, but I did hope he could move my career forward with proper representation because ICM was known for taking on new and young talent.

The Catch 22 was that you needed credits to get an agent and you needed an agent to get auditions which would hopefully lead to acting credits. So

Michael wasn't really able to help me unless I was first able to help myself.

I gave 1,000 percent to my own cause with experience touring with the American Repertory Theatre and off Broadway productions in NYC as well as a couple of walk-ons and a small speaking part on a soap, which is how I got my AFTRA card (American Federation of Radio and Television Artists).

I was working at a West Hollywood eatery called A Votre Sante (To Your Health in French) when my MS rose to the fore and was particularly difficult to get to the bar, which was upstairs a total of 38 steps on an outdoors entrance to the bar.

It was there while working a wrap party for *The Flinstones* movie that John Goodman graciously helped me stock the bar when he saw my difficulties and advised me to leave Hollywood, "There are sharks out there," he said, and that whatever was going on in my body was more important than seeking acting credits.

So that made Spaulding Avenue my last stop out of Dodge, as they say, and eventually led me to my current view of a beautiful Adirondack lake and beach.

I've made a habit all my life wherever I am to call my Mom in Cleveland on New Year's Eve.

I remember calling at 9 p.m. Pacific Time when I was in California where I was traveling enjoying the California weather up the Pacific Coast Highway. It's known locally as the PCH. They also call the state routes 110 and 105 just "the 5" and "the 10."

At the time, I was looking for a good location for a wedding which never came about. It was to be with Bradford Tatum, an actor I met in New York City and came west with to find our mutual fame and fortune.

He has since been in a number of TV shows such as *NYPD Blue* and movies such as *Powder*, but our relationship didn't fare as well. Instead of fame and fortune, he has become known to my friends as "bankruptcy Brad" due to a house we bought and forfeited in Venice Beach. But that, as they say, is another story which I covered previously.

From my family's point of view, the wedding with Brad was quite the fiasco.

Many had purchased tickets to be with me on the west coast, and we never got past the planning stages.

We went so far as having the families meet and having an engagement party with my Mom and sister Debbie in attendance.

Needless to say, when I left Brad for Dana, it put paid to the whole affair and my family were suspicious of any supposed lasting relationships thereafter.

I'm happy to say I proved them wrong when I met my current partner, but that story will come later.

In this photo I am getting into my Ford Tempo which had hand controls when I moved to Upstate New York. This was taken in 1995 by Richard Nilsen.

Chapter 15

Leaving Los Angeles

I always said that I wanted to live where I was happy.

At the end of my time in Los Angeles it became very clear to me that it was time to leave.

The MS was becoming more difficult for me to deal with, so it was time for a change. That involved me leaving LA.

I no longer wanted to deal with all the posturing and game playing that was happening on a daily basis in the entertainment business.

Through my cousin Larry, an ophthalmologist, I learned of a trial for a new drug that was supposed to slow down the process of demyelization around nerves that cause the progression of MS.

The Doctor leading the study was Leslie Weiner, located at USC, but the trial was closed to new patients.

Luckily for me, my cousin knew Dr. Weiner from medical school and arranged for me to get in on the study. It was for what came to be known as Betaseron, one of the "ABC" drugs now in common usage for initial stages of MS called "relapsing-remitting." The "A" stands for a drug called Avonex and the "C" for Copaxone.

Betaseron was the first of the studies with positive outcomes and I was lucky to get in on its usage in the early stages. Trouble is, it only slows the progression and doesn't stop it.

As I've said many times, "My mind is crystal clear and who knows where I would be progression-wise without the Betaseron." Of course, it's impossible to know where that would be.

At the time I was driving a stick shift, VW bug (white convertible, of course, so I could soak up the sun). The license plate was ORAGTOP! Just imagine me trying to shift by pulling my leg up with my hands when they stopped working! Unsafe at any speed! I drove in second gear a lot!

One of my favorite shirts is a light blue, very faded denim button shirt that was given to me after I prodded for it from it's owner. It's another of my "off the owner's back" shirts I have acquired over the years.

I was reminded of how I came to get the shirt as I was watching an episode of "Curb Your Enthusiasm" starring Larry David. If you remember watching *Seinfeld*, he was the co-creator (with Jerry Seinfeld) of that show as well.

I hadn't seen the show, since we don't get premium cable channels like HBO, but reruns are on the *Entertainment on Demand* channel on Time-Warner Cable, and since I'd heard it was a great show and saw some episodes were available on T-W, I decided to give it a shot.

I found myself laughing out loud at the ridiculous situations Larry, Ted Danson and his friends get into, all very reminiscent of the kinds of thing "Seinfeld" was famous for years ago. Basically, ordinary people doing ordinary things wind up in outrageous situations due to poor choices, circumstances and terrible social *faux pas*.

In one episode I watched, Larry and his pals are envious of one of their buddies girlfriend, whose character name is "Cha Cha" played by actress Tia Carrere.

Let me bring this back around to my denim shirt. The shirt was given to me by the owner of "A Votre Sante," (French for "To Your Health") which is a restaurant, actually the *last* restaurant I worked in during my illustrious bartending career.

At the time I worked there, the owner was married to Tia and I often ran into her at the restaurant, where she acted like a very nice, ordinary, regular person. She had no airs or attitude and treated everyone with kindness and grace.

The same wasn't as true about her husband, the restaurant owner, who came down hard on restaurant staff and bartenders in particular.

I just happened to catch him in a relaxed mood one day and when I complimented him on the shirt, he kind of winked and said, "You're a great bartender. It's yours. It's the least I can do."

At the time, my body was actually starting to fail me due to the MS and I was on my way out of the entertainment field in LA. The bar at the restaurant was upstairs, and I remember painstakingly taking each step with my cane to pull myself up to tend bar.

This was the restaurant where "The Flintstones" movie held their wrap party with John Goodman and Rosie O'Donnell and where, as I have written before, Goodman was nice enough to help me stock the bar as well as give me the sound advice to face what was really happening with my body and whether it was worth gambling my health with the sharks in the entertainment business.

So, with this memory, I recommend "Curb Your Enthusiasm," especially if you were a "Seinfeld" fan back in the day since the humor is very similar. And I remember fondly Tia, the restaurant and, at least on that particular day, the owner who parted with his shirt.

At any restaurant where I worked, a big part of the atmosphere was the background music. I often had my own special "mix" of music on tape to plug into the sound system where I worked. That consisted of pop, rock and blues music, which isn't necessarily my favorite.

People often ask me about what kind of music I like. My answer has always been simply, "classical." Specifically, baroque and chamber music.

My love of classical music has roots with my mom and dad. I heard this music a lot as a child growing up. I found it very serene and calming.

High energy runs in my family. It did for my mom and both sisters. I've had to mellow out and slow down with my MS, and classical music centers me so I can deal with not being able to jump up and do whatever I want.

As I often say today, nothing else would have stopped me in my tracks the way MS did. I remember my Dad's waning days at the Cleveland Clinic listening to Itzhak Perlman as he was soloing on the violin with an orchestra in the background. Dad was conducting with his knife and fork as he listened to the music on tape.

The reason I bring this up is I've become an avid listener of WMHT-FM radio, in particular their program called Bach's Lunch. It is an hour of baroque and early music hosted by Chris Wienk from noon until 1 p.m. on weekdays in New York State's Capital District on 89.1.

You can also listen to the streaming audio online at wmht.org.

Shortly after leaving LA and moving to Upstate New York (having met a boyfriend while visiting my Mom at her condo in Florida and he persuading me to accompany him to NY) I had a great experience with a new friend. (I guess you could say one favor the "new boyfriend" did for me was introduce me to a very nice lady named Sunny.

Her name is ironic in that I love the sun so much to this day.)

One of my fondest and most cherished memories was when my new friend Sunny took me to see Perlman at Saratoga Performing Arts Center. This was back in the mid 1990s and I was still walking with a cane.

The thing is, Perlman is also handicapped, walking with two canes called Canadian Crutches due to having had polio.

So when I asked if I could go back stage to meet him and tell him about my father's dying days listening to his music, Perlman graciously granted me an audience.

I would like to say I asked him some great

questions and we had a great discussion, but in fact I told him about my Dad's dying days and was too emotional to say much else.

Perlman patted my shoulder and said, "It's OK. I understand." And I think he really did.

So, whenever I hear violin music as beautiful as that played on Bach's Lunch, I think back on my Dad, my time with Perlman and a peace comes over me.

I hope you get to listen in and find the same wonder and peace that I do.

This photo shows me in an amusement car ride in 1972 with
my adoptive father, Joe Spira, who sadly died in 1987.

Chapter 16

East Coast Boyfriend, Looking for a New Home & Getting Wheels

As I said before, I wound up moving to Upstate New York with a guy I met in Florida while visiting with my Mom at her condo in Siesta Key.

It seems much of my moving across the country had to do with whatever boyfriend I was with at the time and not due to my own personal choices.

That was true both of my moving from NYC to LA and from Florida to Upstate New York. It happens that both moves turned out OK, but they weren't really planned.

Oh, and both boyfriends who inspired the moves turned out to fizzle out.

The bottom line is, I found my home here in Upstate New York with a lot of peace here in the Adirondack Mountains.

And the transition took place with a total change from pursuing acting to expressing myself through writing a column, Kathryn's Korner, from whence comes the title of this memoir.

It came about like this: My friend Lynn Cirillo (actually my previous boyfriend's mother), came up with the title when I floated the idea by her. I was looking for an outlet for my creative energy that had gone into acting auditions and attempts and decided to try my hand at column writing.

I think at the time (it was early 1995) I was reading a Dave Barry humor column and loved the matter-of-fact silliness of his humor. Thinking about all my experiences in "Hollyweird," I thought that I could speak about my past pursuits. There had been an ad in the local newspaper for a newspaper reporter and I asked the editor at the time for a job as a columnist rather than a reporter.

He asked me if I had any sample columns. I admit I lied and said my copies had been lost in flight from LA, but I would write up a sample, which I drove home and did that day. I bought a word processor (remember those?) at Office Max and wrote up what I thought was a hilarious column.

Looking back, that first column was too long, full of unnecessary thoughts and lacked a focus. But for some reason, the editor at the time decided to take me on and the column ran to my great delight.

A later editor suggested I concentrate more on my experiences in pursuing acting, which gave me more focus, and the column has now been in print for more than 20 years.

Along the way, many people have been "in my korner." I have no end of people to thank, from those who inspired the experiences when I was chasing my dream to those who still read my column to this day.

I don't really want to dwell on the false starts with boyfriends, but they did bring about what came next. When "the boyfriend" and I broke up (the one I moved to Upstate New York for, that is) I was driving around in my 1989 Ford Tempo in search of a place to live.

Actually, how I bought the Tempo is a story in itself.

I moved first from LA to Cleveland where my Mom lived at the time. It was actually my parents' home in Beachwood, after they had moved from University Heights where I grew up. (Quick aside here. My Mom and biological father divorced when I was in second grade and my Mom married Joe Spira, who adopted me as his own and I called him Dad throughout his life.

He sadly passed away about the time I was diagnosed with MS. I have since renewed my relationship with my father and we keep in touch as of this writing.)

But back to the Ford Tempo, the last of my self-driven cars.

From a Ragtop to a 'Chauffeur-Driven' Van

My first car was a 1966 Volkswagen Beetle complete with chrome bumpers and an old-fashioned AM radio. But when I got to California chasing my dream of acting, I wanted a car to go with the Southern California lifestyle, and the most important thing about that was that it be a convertible. I bought the 1978 VW Beetle in Venice Beach and it even came with a vanity plate that said "ORAGTOP." (In California, the license plate stays with the car when you sell it.)

Now, at the time I didn't know that "rag top" was slang for convertible.

I bring this up because as I was going through old paperwork I came upon my old California registration with the plate on it.

In between these two beetles I had a 1972 green VW Square-back while I lived in New York City. Having a car in NYC was a pain: trying to find parking, paying tolls and doing alternate side of the street parking. Sometimes much of the driving I did was moving my car from side to side so the street cleaners could work.

I remember seeing drivers running from side to side of the street moving their cars so they wouldn't be ticketed and towed or booted. Getting your car out of hock might cost $100, a lot for me back then. You'd see people running the street in their pajamas or half hung over or in my case, coming home on the subway from partying all night.

As my MS progressed in L.A., I found it harder and harder to shift the Beetle and had to use my hand to pick up my leg to work the clutch and shift. I would drive in second gear period, just so I wouldn't have to shift gears. I remember I loved hills where I could coast in neutral.

I've told you about the actor John Goodman seeing me struggle with MS and telling me the town was full of sharks and it was time to get out. About this time I had just broken up with my latest boyfriend and decided to move back home to Cleveland where I searched the papers for an automatic that would be easier to drive and found one in my Mom's morning Cleveland Plain Dealer. It was downtown in a poor neighborhood and my mother made me promise to dicker on the price and not to make a quick decision. Instead, I told the owner I'd take it without even test driving it. It was a 1989 Ford Tempo and Vocational and Educational Services for Individuals with Disabilities (VESID) put hand controls in it when I moved to Fulton County in Upstate

New York and I drove it until I couldn't use the hand controls either.

(These days, I'm "chauffeured" in a handicapped-accessible van wherever I need to go. I'd rather be able to drive myself, but at least I can still get around. Of course, I'd rather not have MS, but I've always tried to look on the bright side. I've always maintained I gained more than I lost. Nothing else would have made me stop and smell the roses.)

So I was driving around in my Ford Tempo with hand controls near where my now former boyfriend lived and I saw a sign in front of an older home in the small town of Northville. The sign was on a white cardboard box with red painted letters stating, "Free rent to rite person." Yeah, "rite."

So I pulled over, struggled up the steps to the porch with my fold-out cane and knocked on the door. Who met me was an old man named Seymour who basically was the oldest man I had ever met thus far. He seemed perfectly harmless, just lonely, as his wife had recently been moved into a health-care facility due to her dementia.

Considering my finances, or lack thereof, I decided to take Seymour up on his generous offer and he even helped me move along with his elderly neighbor, a dear man named Chan. Seymour's brother, John, a carpenter, made me a beautiful custom-made desk for writing which I treasure to this day. So all in all it was a good experience.

Seymour even took offense to my former boyfriend as we were moving since "the boyfriend" felt I was moving into unknown territory, but as usual I was stubborn and did as I wanted. Once again, to quote Blanche in *A Streetcar Named Desire*, "I have always relied upon the kindness of strangers."

Me with my first VW in 1976.

My sister, Linda, niece Jen, nephew Josh, brother-in-law, Howard, and me at Seymour's house in Northville in 1995.

Chapter 17

Northville, The Pink Flamingo & The Bakery Garden

After moving into a room at Seymour's, I would get up and try to jog around Northville (actually wound up walking with my fold-up cane), I found some new favorite places like The Bakery Garden for fresh bagels and muffins while sitting on their wicker furniture which they had for sale there.

Lunches were often at a place called the Pink Flamingo with the obvious lawn decoration for which the restaurant was named. I might hang out with a new friend Kelly or Sunny and would daily drive to the Jewish Community Center in Gloversville about 30 miles away where I would swim and try to keep up my exercise program.

I also started attending an MS support group at the

local Family Counseling Center, also in Gloversville.

I didn't last very long at this support group as I often was the cheerleader for the group which drained on me. The rest of the women there were in the "Oh, poor me" phase of their disability while I was trying to ignore it as much as possible. Their viewpoint was something I didn't want to go through. I never did go through the phase of "poor me" as part of my disability. Some might call this denial, but I think of it as positive thinking.

It was at the end of one of these meetings that the five women I was walking out with all using canes and a little boy came up to ask what our "club" was all about. I simply responded, "This is a club you don't want to be a part of."

I think it was that same evening that a guy approached me, said he recognized me from my picture in the newspaper over my weekly column and asked if I'd like to come to his writing seminar called "Writers Block" that met monthly, also in Gloversville. I hastily said, "Yeah, sure," and then proceeded to blow him off. After all, I was still living on my own, but was badly scarred from my last relationship.

Richard (also known as "Herman" in my weekly column) ultimately tracked me down several weeks later and asked me to attend a different writers group in Saratoga Springs to which I replied yes and we agreed to meet at a park-and-ride lot in nearby Vails Mills.

I wanted to make sure his car had air conditioning, as my MS was very sensitive to heat and when he replied he did indeed have AC the deal was sealed.

That night we chatted non-stop all the hour-long drive to Saratoga, through dinner out and the Writer's Circle group which was then meeting at Uncommon Grounds coffee house and all the way back to the park-and-ride lot. After we drove back I said to Richard, "This was like being up all night huffing blow and needing 'ludes to come down afterwards. It was a real natural high."

We had a quick embrace and kiss and I drove home. I remember I called my friend Nancy in California and said I had met this guy, who was nice, but definitely not "the one." At which point, Nancy replied, after dropping the phone, "Oh, shit! Every guy you meet is 'the one.' This time you say he isn't and I'll be flying out to your wedding!"

I replied, "Nance, I think I know what I'm talking about when I say he is *not* the one!" She simply said, "I'll see you soon!"

Of course, Nancy's words turned out to be prophetic, and she did indeed fly out to what turned out to be our union service, April 21, 1996. But before then, Richard and I had not only gotten "close," he had proposed to me at our favorite "pit stop" on the way to Northville, an antique shop called "The Red Barn," and I had said "No! You can't afford me!"

You see, at this time I was on some expensive medication that had come through a research study by Dr. Leslie Weiner out of University of Southern California which was covered by my disability status. If we got married, I was pretty sure his health insurance or lack thereof would have to pay the, at the time, $36,000 per year tab, and he just didn't have that kind of high-paying job or that great insurance.

We confirmed my suspicions with the local heads of social services Medicaid and Social Security. So, a union service it was meant to be! And as Richard often likes to say, "We invited friends, family, the church and the synagogue, but not the State of New York — and they weren't missed!"

One thing was missing, according to my family who had lived through the "runaway bride" thing in California. Where was the ring?

I sit in my power chair along side my handicapped accessible van in 2007.

Ralph Castiglione, who designed our rings stands with my friend, actor/playwright Nancy Baker, who flew in from California for our union service. Bottom: I am on my scooter and Richard walks along side me at Lanzi's On The Lake after the union service in April 1996.

Chapter 18

The Ring Thing

Richard had a friend who owned a local jewelry shop in Gloversville called Matty the Jeweler after the original owner, now run by his son Ralph.

I went with Richard to meet Ralph to discuss what kind of ring we wanted.

I was very specific when explaining what I wanted.

With my usual joking manner, I told Ralph what I wanted was to "take this guy to the cleaners!"

After Ralph stopped laughing, he said that suiting a diamond and ring to me was going to be much harder now that he knew my personality.

I said I didn't want a traditional solitaire setting, or for that matter, any traditional setting. What I wanted was an antique filigree type ring of platinum or white gold and a stone that would be eye catching but not ostentatious.

At that, Ralph pulled out an antique setting he had acquired at an estate sale in Saratoga Springs and it was perfect.

We just had to find the right stone to place in the setting. Ralph pulled out three stones of three sizes.

The first was so small it dropped right through the setting. I said that would never do. And the largest one was something Richard said he just couldn't afford.

But like Goldilocks and the three bears, we found the middle one to be "just right."

Once the ring was settled and on my finger, I could confidently call my family and make arrangements.

The thing was, I had a Jewish background and Richard had a Christian background. So what kind of service, even a union service, should we have?

See, at the time, the Rabbi at the local synagogue (there was only one synagogue in the area) was too conservative to encourage a "mixed marriage" in his view.

Fortunately, Richard was attending a Methodist Church where the pastor there didn't hold as strict views and who was happy to administer our vows, although he said he couldn't say the whole "man and wife" thing because it was a union service.

Happily, Pastor Steve Clunn also was open to having some Jewish traditions as part of the ceremony so everyone could be accommodated.

By that time I had gotten to know the pastor and had attended Richard's church several times. He was not only open to doing a union service with a "mixed" couple. He had even administered a heartfelt divorce for an elderly couple who would gain social security benefits if they were no longer legally married!

This was a guy who cared more for a person's well-being than following every silly rule in the book.

May his tribe increase!

Anyway, friends we had made together over a six-month period helped put together a chuppah (literally "canopy") with a crystal goblet (to be smashed by the groom) supplied by our jeweler friend, Ralph.

Another friend, Gene Horn, spoke about the meaning of the broken glass (covered in a cloth napkin so no broken shards injure anyone). The tradition apparently has a variety of meanings. Gene's narration included the following:

The most widespread meaning attached to the glass-smashing ritual is that it symbolizes the destruction of the Temple in Jerusalem in 70AD.

As the Temple functioned as the centre of worship in Judaism, its destruction has been devastating to the Jewish people. By remembering this national sadness during the joyous festivities of a wedding, Jews "set Jerusalem above [their] highest joy" (Psalm 137).

This celebration of Jewish identity is seen as auspicious for the new couple, placing the beginning of their married life within the framework of the joys and sorrows of Jews throughout history.

Friends we had made separately and as a couple all participated in the service.

There were many things we hadn't made provision for, from photography and music to videoing and transportation to and from the service.

Even our honeymoon accommodations were supplied by friends as you will see in my next chapter.

Pastor Steve Clunn hears our vows in April 1996.

From left, Elizabeth, Lauren, Josh, Jennie, my nieces and
nephew at the union service April 1996.

Sisters three: Debbie, me and Linda at our union service.

Top: I and Richard stand at our union service in April 1996.
Bottom: My nieces Jennie, Elizabeth and Lauren stand next
to me at our union service in April 1996.

Chapter 19

A Union Service &
A Mixup of Dresses

I found a beautiful dress at a boutique in Johnstown called Sally's Naturally You, unfortunately no longer in business.

Actually, Richard had bought a couple of dresses for me to attend a couple weddings I had previously planned to attend with my former boyfriend. You could say he kind of scored some "kismet" or at least some points with me for that. As I recall, we then went together to the boutique to pick out the dress for the union service.

Sally, the owner, was very nice and helpful, and in fact, was a friend of Richard's, wound up coming to the event and even supplied a limo as transport and a night at a local bed and breakfast at The Olde Knox Mansion, an historic landmark hereabouts. And the dress wasn't even that expensive!

We had become friends with the owners of Lanzi's On The Lake, a restaurant owned by the Lanzi brothers, and set the service for April 21, 1996.

The scene was beautiful as it overlooked the Great Sacandaga Lake and we were hoping for good weather, which is always unpredictable in the Northeast, especially in April.

In talking it over with Chris Lanzi and his brother, Lou, we decided to have the event inside if the weather was too cold, or outside on the off chance it was warm enough.

Well, guess what, the morning of the event Chris Lanzi called to ask first, "Are you sure you are going through with this?" That was tongue-in-cheek because he knew my past as a "runaway bride." In fact, Richard took the phone to ask jokingly if the bartender was male or female. (You may remember the last time I was engaged I wound up running off with the bartender, Dana, who I was smitten with.)

Chris responded, the bartender was female and the weather looked good enough to have the service outside although the dinner (underwritten by my Mom) would be served inside to the approximately 70 guests attending.

We had made no plans for photography or any other of the ordinary wedding type observances, but once again, there were many people "in my corner" and several people came with cameras as well as our Northville neighbor, Chan, who came with a video camera and made a beautiful recording of the service and dinner afterward as a wedding gift.

The only fly in the ointment was that the lady we had asked to sing at our wedding showed up with the same dress I was wearing! (Who wears a white dress to someone else's wedding?)

At this point of frustration, my sister, Debbie stated, "This is what big sisters are for!" She went to talk with the lady, who, to give her her due, graciously put a rain coat over the culprit dress over the protestations of her new husband (they had just been married the week previous and we had actually been at their wedding.)

Anyway, our friend, Gene Horn, gave the toast and history of the breaking of the glass, as I spoke about in the last chapter and other friends Anne, Lou, Jean and Kelly put up the hoopah, which they had borrowed from our local synagogue (thanks Debbie!) and finally our thanks to Pastor Steve Clunn who did a beautiful service while avoiding the words "man and wife" as well as reading a great quote from Kalil Gibran's *The Prophet*.

The service ended with a beautiful Native American flute rendition by Richard's friend, Franklyn, and we all retired to the dinner with prayers, blessings and the usual champagne toast wherein my Mom made sure every glass was filled no matter the cost! (I think she wore out two credit cards that day!)

After the dinner and some more impromptu photos, we were whisked off by limo (thank you Sally) to the Inn at the Bridge in Northville after a very satisfying union service.

Top left: Clockwise from left are Jennie, Howard, my sister Linda, and Josh Bliss pose at our union service.

Top right: I and Richard pose with the Great Sacandaga Lake behind us at our union service.

Above: I give my mother a hug for making our union service possible.

Richard, me, Aunt Margie, Mom, Aunt Renee and Uncle
Erry sit for a group shot at Mom's in Thanksgiving of 1999.

Richard's camp is shown after being re-habbed with insulation, A.C. and new steel roof, Anderson casement windows,
cathedral ceiling, new wiring and plumbing.

Chapter 20

Finding a Place of Our Own: Sacandaga, Canada & Caroga Lakes

We were still in Northville where I had been "renting" a room from an elderly man named Seymour who offered the place for "Free to 'rite' person."

But when Richard came into the picture, it was weird for both of us to be living with this elderly (often cantankerous) man who seemed to be more upset when Richard moved in with me. We needed to find a place of our own on very little money.

At the time, Richard was directing Big Brothers Big Sisters in our county and asked me to be on the board. I was already volunteering as a board member on the Fulton County Planning Board and Jewish Community Center (which is no more; a pity). So with me living on disability as the MS progressed, our combined assets didn't amount to much.

Richard was living in his inherited family "camp" at Caroga Lake, which had been partially insulated but had no running water and was very small with low ceilings and a wood stove for heat. When he took me there I had to use the toilet which wasn't properly bolted to the floor and had to be flushed with a pail of water. Not good!

At this time I was still walking with a cane but was somewhat unsteady on my feet. I made it plain to Richard that a seasonal camp, no matter what memories he had of growing up summers there, would in no way be a place for me to stay unless radical surgery was performed!

The walls were just clapboard over 2-by-4s with fiberglass insulation between the studs.

Grotesque!

The insulation was pink and showed along the studs because they had been placed before there was a standardized sizing (now 16 inches I think) so the rolled insulation had to be cut to fit. (Richard showed me the markings in the base of the chimney showing the original building was made 1935).

Anyway, we learned of a cute little place through my friend Sunny in nearby Mayfield on the Great Sacandaga Lake.

It was within our price range with a cute picket fence and adjoining garage which would allow me to get in and out of my car out of the weather with a short single step up into the cabin's kitchen.

There was even a basement for storage since the little cabin was quite small, about the same size as Richard's 600-square-foot camp.

In order to get a bank loan, we had to get the place inspected and had a local engineering firm do that.

The engineer stated that in no uncertain terms, "You said you wanted to be close to the lake? With this cabin you may well end up *in* the lake!"

Since the cabin was on a hillside overlooking the Sacandaga, it was a short trip down to the lake (or muddy shoreline depending on how much the Black River/Hudson River Regulating District* decided the lake should be lowered at any time).

---

* The Black River/Hudson River Regulating District is the governing organization that controls the Great Sacandaga Lake. The Sacandaga River was dammed in 1930, flooding the Sacandaga Valley and creating what then was known as the Sacandaga Reservoir. Despite the growth of a summer vacation area around the shore of what now is known as the Great Sacandaga Lake, the District regulates the level of the water to use for hydro-electric power and to control flooding downstream at Albany of the Hudson River. This means that the man-made lake's level fluctuates wildly in the spring and summer, making some properties shrink and causing potential instability of structures.

The engineer showed us that the basement foundation was "rotten," as he put it. Seems a lot of concrete blocks were made up of inferior cement during wartime and when moisture got into the cement (a sure thing with any basement) the cement disintegrated. The engineer actually was able to stick a screwdriver through the basement wall and dig out rotten cement with his fingers!

Once the inspection was made, the findings went into the real estate report and the next buyer reaped the results of our paid inspection by getting the place for about half the original asking price. (Richard later visited the cabin which was bought by an acquaintance who shored up the basement, put drainage around it and closed it in to make a very livable basement bedroom and sitting area which looked out on the lake. It just took half-again the price of the place to do it!)

Anyway, we next looked into a camp on Canada Lake a couple miles north of Richard's camp. (All seasonal bungalows in the Adirondacks take on the moniker of "camp" after the "great camps" of the wealthy owners who first established the term in the early 1900s.)

This camp had been owned by a cousin of Richard's and was for sale by his widow after he passed away from cancer.

Unfortunately, this place also was seasonal and would have to be re-vamped for year-round use.

Since Richard already owned his camp, it seemed cheaper to just make that a year-round cabin while we stayed in Northville until the job was finished.

Richard's brother-in-law did a wonderful job of putting in new wiring and copper plumbing as well as a new circuit breaker box. A friend in construction named Mario did the sheet rock and Richard peeled back the old linoleum to reveal wooden floors which he took a sander to and painted with clear polyurethane. We got an above-ground water pump for the dug well (which tended to run dry in summer) and put in a small 20-gallon used water heater.

I had a problem when the well ran dry and Richard tried, unsuccessfully, to make it deeper and more reliable. I actually used to take showers with a flower sprinkler and water from a local spring!

Not what I was used to!

Funny story: One day when Mario was fixing the roof and changing it over from asphalt shingle to metal, I asked him how hard it would be to take out the cramped upstairs bedrooms which I couldn't access anyway and make cathedral ceilings. Richard was in town at work and Mario stated it would take no time at all and took a wrecking bar and hammer to the upstairs in miraculously short time.

When Richard came home that evening, Mario mischievously told him to, "Take a look inside and see what you think."

Richard was astonished, both because we had taken the initiative to remove the small upstairs and because the result was much more open and full of light.

We did leave a loft bedroom over the master bedroom just big enough for a queen box spring and mattress with no frame, so we could accommodate guests if needed.

This change not only opened things up and made the whole tiny cabin seem much bigger, it seemed to modernize the look of the place.

Due to my disability with MS I also was able to access funding through VESID (Vocational and Educational Services for Individuals with Disabilities).

They put in ramped access, Anderson double-glazed, casement windows and handicapped accessible bathroom and kitchen fixtures.

The place was really starting to shape up!

However, at this time we still had no running water and in talking with local people found the best solution was to drill a well.

We contacted Adirondack Well Drilling at the advice of a friend and they came with a huge derrick and well drilling rig finding enough water at 96 feet in depth.

We now had reliable water.

And oh, heat was important in the Adirondacks as well, so we put in both a wood stove and through-the-wall LP stove, neither of which needed electricity in case the power went out.

I am holding my beloved cat Sam-the-Man at the re-habbed
Nilsen Camp in 1997.

Chapter 21

Moving Day

The whole process of fixing up the seasonal camp for year-round use took much longer than I wanted and we finally were able to make our move in March 1997.

Trouble is, we didn't have our furniture and appliances installed yet, or even purchased, so we decided to do the purchasing and moving all at once!

We made a caravan of cars, vans, trailer and such with friends from our union service and Richard's church helping with the move.

Along the way from Northville to Caroga Lake, we stopped in to a second-hand furniture store and two other places to pick up a refrigerator, gas stove, dining table and chairs and wicker furniture I had previously purchased at the Bakery Garden.

Everyone was very patient and helpful as we made our move (about 25 miles one way) in two trips and all in one day!

I already had it planned out in my mind where everything was to go, and with the small floor space in the new digs there wasn't a lot of room for innovation anyway.

The refrigerator had a bottom drawer freezer, so I could easily see from my wheelchair just what was in it.

Richard and I each had a queen sized mattress from before we were together. One went upstairs in the loft overlooking our living area and the other barely fit in the bedroom downstairs along with a dresser and small closet.

A new shower stall was fitted into the bathroom along with a handicapped accessible commode, ramped access door to the outside and sink I could roll my manual wheelchair under to use. (At that time I was able to use my arms and hands to get around although my legs had pretty much stopped working.)

The lyrics from Crosby, Stills, Nash and Young's *Déjà vu* album come to mind.

This was "our house, a very, very nice house."

A kitten had been reserved with Richard's daughter — a ginger, male cat I named Sam — and we soon added a Dalmatian female pooch named Moxie. Two more lovable animals would be hard to find.

We had our "Little Cabin in the Big Woods" of the Adirondacks with lake rights that remained inaccessible to me due to a steep incline down a hill about 100 yards distant.

Not only did VESID underwrite accessible renovations to the camp, they also opted to underwrite my finishing the bachelor's degree I had left when I joined the American Repertoire Theater Company after my junior year at Indiana University.

I decided to enroll in Empire State College in their distance learning program, a concept that was new to me but has since become quite common.

I was able to matriculate with all my voice, theater and dance credits by majoring in "expressive arts" to continue with my now two-year-old job writing columns for the local Sunday edition of The Leader-Herald.

A local furniture maker designed a beautiful, wooden, wheelchair accessible computer desk for me and I was able to continue my college studies via telephone and computer without actually attending a classroom setting.

VESID also underwrote a voice activated computer program called Dragon Dictate to help me when my fingers refused to respond properly and I began submitting articles to magazines with eventual publications in Many Waters (a literary arm of Empire State College) and New Mobility Magazine.

Besides my continued publications in The Sunday Leader-Herald, an old friend who had a web-based financial site offered to provide my own web site for my columns which continues as of this writing at www.kathrynskorner.com, and I also send my column to an out-of-town list of readers via email.

It seemed my visions of fame and recognition had finally been realized in a small but meaningful way through my writings where they hadn't ever really been realized through my acting efforts.

One example of my local notoriety came about when Richard took my Ford Tempo into a garage for a wheel alignment.

When the mechanic asked why there were hand controls in the Tempo which Richard obviously didn't need, he said they were for me, Kathryn Spira, because my legs didn't work.

George, the owner of the garage, backed out of his adjoining office on his wheeled office chair and asked, "And how are Sam and Moxie doing?"

You never knew who might be reading my columns to the point they even remembered the names of my pets!

About this time I realized my driving, even with hand controls, was a risk to myself and others. So my much-loved Ford Tempo with hand controls was sold and Richard acquired a handicapped accessible Chrysler mini-van with ramped entry.

Richard had an older Jeep Cherokee that was so

dented and rusty it looked like it might have been rolled in a previous life.

As he was backing out of the driveway one day to go to work and a personal care aide named Kelly was driving in, they collided, scraping his Jeep along the side of her Ford Bronco.

As they each leaped out of their SUVs to see what damage was done, they both burst out laughing because each vehicle was in such bad shape you couldn't tell where they had collided!

Richard, his daughter, Cara, and I sit at my Dad's house in
California in 1998.

Chapter 22

Back to California With Cara & A Non-Scheduled Stop at Raton

In the summer of 1998, Richard's daughter, Cara, planned to go out to California State University at Fullerton where she had been accepted into their Master of Fine Arts program.

She didn't want to make the drive alone and so we signed up to take her. Since the Jeep Cherokee was on its last legs, we were in the market for a new SUV, one that could pull her VW Jetta all the way to California.

We had heard good things about Nissan Pathfinders so went to the local Nissan dealer and tried one out.

Sad to say, we found it tinny and low on power.

In the back of the lot, ready to be sold at the state car auction was an Eddie Bauer edition of a Ford Explorer at half the price of the used Pathfinder we had tried out.

The salesman we spoke to tried to talk us out of the lower-priced vehicle, but we took it for a spin and loved the ride, solid construction and overall feel of the vehicle.

When we went inside to sign up for it, the salesman made the mistake of being cute and writing a number on a slip of paper and sliding it face-down across his desk to Richard.

I admit I let slip a choice swear word as I told him in no uncertain terms that I would be making the decision on the vehicle! Richard laughed and we got the price down to our affordable limit.

The Explorer wound up being a good choice for the trip, with extra power and a ride like a limo. Also, the air conditioning was excellent, something my heat-sensitive MS required.

Now, for the trip itself.

I'm not even sure where to begin.

The major car accident we had in New Mexico?

No, that would make no sense.

Well, then.

The beginning seems to be of tremendous logic to

even me.

My plan would have been to ship her car out by train and fly out. She could stay and enjoy school, the beach and the beauty of the West Coast. We would leave her there and fly back to the serenity of the Adirondack Mountains, aka home, and everyone would be happy.

Sounds perfect, right? I thought so.

Turns out Richard and his daughter had *way* different plans.

They wanted to drive towing her Jetta on what I now know as a tow dolly. I didn't really want to hear this great plan. I'd driven out there across the country when I was in search of fame as an actress.

At the time, I wanted to drive just to say I'd done it.

Well, now I can say I've done it twice.

Additionally, I can also say I drove back east, because the first time when I tired of it out there I flew back.

And so it began.

June 28th, Richard picked up the tow dolly with our new-to-us, used Explorer.

Richard wisely took out "trip insurance" for the Jetta.

At home, I packed bags with the help of an aide

and made sandwiches for the trip. That evening, Cara drove up and they hook the Jetta up in the pouring rain.

June 26th at 5 a.m. was blast-off time to drive to Chicago and spend the weekend with my sister and her family there.

Then we left on the 28th and drove 20 hours straight through to Denver.

People asked me if the drive out was hard on me.

My answer was, "What's the diff? I'm sitting all the time anyway in my wheelchair." That's the amount of attention I'll allow the MS.

Yeah, yeah, I know. I don't kid myself.

But there's this thing called life that must go on.

And that's *way* bigger than anything that can be abbreviated with two letters.

After an over-night in a motel in Denver, we made a quick stop in Colorado Springs, which happens to be the home base of Bookstore Journal, a magazine Richard did book reviews for over several years. He'd only communicated with them by email and got to meet the editor and staff in person for a change. Next pit stop was my aunt, uncle and cousins in Phoenix who I hadn't seen in, like, forever.

So we're traveling south on U.S. Route 25 through New Mexico when all of a sudden we're up on two wheels on one side then the other. I'm looking out the windshield thinking, "Well, this is it."

Then I hear a loud crash and we are still. I do a quick inventory, see we are all alive, thank God, look out the window and see the only thing between us and about a quarter mile drop into a canyon are guard rails. Never before have I been so happy to see a guardrail!

It seems there was a malfunction with the tow dolly as it went over a frost heave and, according to Richard, the tow dolly "jack knifed" and pulled us into the guard rails against our wills.

In the process, Cara's Jetta was totaled and we parted company with it in a salvage yard there in New Mexico. The Explorer had a bad case of "road rash" on the passenger side, but otherwise was drivable with not even a turn signal lens broken.

Since Cara's belongings were all packed into her empty Jetta, we had to unload her car at the salvage yard and buy a cartopper container to fit everything into one vehicle.

In we went to my extended family in Phoenix where I was amazed at how fast the city had grown. My cousin Bob stated that when he had first moved there, they were 10 miles outside the city limits. Now, the city limits were ten miles past his house! That's a 20-mile radius increase over the approximately 20-plus years they had lived there.

We also weren't used to the dry heat of the dessert, where the most expensive utility was water! My cousins had something called a "swamp cooler" for cooling the house, since they didn't turn on the AC until it was *really* hot in July and August.

At midnight, Richard and I were so hot in that climate we weren't used to (it was 98°F!) that we decided to take a dip in their backyard swimming pool.

Cousin Bob warned us to bring towels for the chill that would come after the dip, which we could hardly imagine. But he was right! The "wicking" action of the dessert-dry air on our wet bodies once out of the pool brought goose bumps even at 98°F!

We started off early the next morning and made it to L.A. late in the evening where we stayed with my biological father and his lovely partner Regina.

I refer to my "natural" father since that is what he is, however I was raised by my adoptive father Joe, whom I called Dad all the while he was alive. He sadly passed away in 1987, but encouraged me to reconnect to my natural father, saying it was "only natural" to do so. I now can refer to my natural father as "Dad" since we have reconnected for many years now.

It was wild seeing he and Reg both. What was wild was seeing my friends out there. They all came to me. I told them I was done driving. If they wanted to see me, they were doing the driving.

When I say it was wild seeing my friends, I don't mean wild as in crazy, I mean wild like weird. It was as if five years had passed for me, but no time had passed on their end.

In other words, it was like they were stuck in a freeze frame.

Maybe it was as simple as being removed from the world of actors.

See, we were always bemoaning our plight as unemployed, under thanked, overworked in "means-to-an-end" jobs while being misunderstood and give me a light for my millionth cigarette as I listen to the blues type.

Who knows?

When I asked Regina if I was ever like that, she stated simply, "You were worse!"

Here I am getting my B.A. diploma from the dean of Empire State College in 2001 at graduation in Saratoga Springs, NY.

Chapter 23

Visits From Mom, Giff, Linda, Debbie, Mary & a B.A.

In April of 2000 I turned 40 and Richard threw a birthday party for me at Lanzi's On The Lake where we had our union service in 1996. My sister, Linda, was able to come as well as my Mom and best friend from high school, Carol Gifford.

Giff had stayed overnight after the birthday party and my Mom and sister Linda had stayed at Holiday Inn in Johnstown, about 15 miles southeast of us. Giff stayed in the sleeping loft and when she awoke the next morning, looked outside her window and exclaimed, "Where do you people live!"

Apparently there had been a sudden drop in temperature and we had heavy, wet snow come down to the tune of 14 inches overnight!

Richard asked Giff to help him move a tree out of the driveway, which she assumed was a joke. No joke! We had lost power and there were trees down all over due to the heavy, wet snow.

Luckily, we had our four-wheel-drive Explorer to power out of the driveway, but there were so many trees down that we had to take secondary roads to get to town and have brunch with my Mom and sister. It is always an adventure here in the Adirondacks!

A B.A. from Empire State in 2001

I finally became a college graduate in 2001.

And I am so proud of this achievement after all these years. Commencement was Oct. 14, 2001 in Saratoga Springs; Canfield Casino in Congress Park, to be exact.

It certainly was a long road since I began my studies in 1978 at Indiana University in Bloomington, Indiana. I had left school after my junior year as I had gotten hired for a professional acting troupe called ART Reach as an outreach program of the American Repertoire Theatre.

It was always in the back of my mind to go back and finish, but I became immersed in my quest for fame both in New York City then Los Angeles. Until my MS literally stopped me in my tracks, I hadn't taken the time to research my educational options.

Empire State College has turned out to be a great thing for me as well as for most of the students I met at graduation. It was weird not knowing any of my fellow students until graduation day and it was wonderful finally meeting my advisor and many of the faculty and administration.

We began with a lovely brunch where we first met fellow students and faculty with whom we'd been working over the phone, Internet and mail. After brunch, we all headed down the street to the Canfield Casino where all the students donned our caps and gowns.

The college had given each of the female graduates corsages with school colors. I gotta tell you, keeping that cap on was a major undertaking. My mom and one of my sisters came as well as Richard and his cousin Dave and I have to tell you that the ceremony was absolutely magical. I was so proud, and still am, to have been a part of it.

So much so, that after having met the Dean of Graduate Studies, I considered going forward to pursue a graduate degree in creative writing after a brief hiatus to gather my thoughts and prepare a focus for my studies.

I thought it would be the following summer, but it never came about.

Richard and I pose in front of our beach at West Caroga
Lake in 2012.

Chapter 24

Our Very Own Beach House

One day late in the summer of 2000 when we were driving to town along the lake, I spied a For Sale sign along an empty lot that seemed to contain a private beach! I yelled to Richard to stop the car.

He thought I was having a problem and had to pee!

Actually, I wanted to stop and investigate the place that was for sale.

See, the camp we had renovated was cozy and nice, but it was 100 yards from the lake, through trees and down a steep hill. That was totally inaccessible to me in my wheelchair! We had tried getting there once down a neighbor's driveway that came near the lake, but it was so hard that we determined never to try that again.

So we went back to the camp and called the realtor, who explained the lot was owned by a single, elderly man in an adult home. He had no family and the proceeds were to go towards his living expenses. We were about to offer about 80 percent of the asking, when a neighbor who had previously thought about buying the property told us the lawyers handling the sale would be willing to take half the asking, a real bargain and one we could actually afford with an equity loan against the camp.

Now, in 2001, banks were much friendlier when it came to loans than in later years. We were able to get a construction loan, Richard acted as his own general contractor and we asked our friend, Carl, to design a home with lots of glass looking toward the lake view, cathedral ceilings, lots of wood, a balcony loft and all accessible by wheelchair. That was no small feat, but he did it! He also threw in an alcove for wheelchair van access out of the weather.

Before we even closed on the purchase, in the fall of 2000, Richard built a ramp and deck on the beach so I could get to the beach in my wheelchair. This was definitely shaping up to be our dream house!

We called back the guys who had drilled our well at the camp and they drilled one for us here at the new site. A local excavator Richard had known all his life graded the property, brought in six truckloads of topsoil fill and dug a septic system and leach field. We also had various trees which obstructed the view and so we had them taken down. When we were hesitant about cutting down trees, the tree surgeon pointed out that each of the pine trees had been struck by lightening in the past. His quote was, "I can take them down cheaply now or I can take them out of your living room at great expense later!"

So we took him at his word and had the trees taken down and hauled away. We had hoped to use some of the wood on the property for green board and batten from a local mill, but found the trees were so eaten up with insects and lightening strikes that it wasn't worth it. We believed him and let the wood go. (A local furniture maker who took some of the wood did make us an end table in return for the wood.)

I had Richard start the tongue-in-groove flooring in the master bedroom because I had ordered a four poster bed from Eddie Bauer and needed the floor finished so it could be set up. A team from the Eddie Bauer Home Store came to do the job as part of their service. (I see where Eddie Bauer Home Stores no longer exist as of this writing, perhaps because of extravagant services like this.)

Richard and I stayed up until midnight every night for the last three months of 2001 to finish the interior. We put the last coat of polyurethane on the floors the night before we moved in and on Dec. 29

made the move from the camp, since we had a buyer for the camp who wanted to move in Jan. 1.

So we finally had our beach house and the first night we stayed there it seemed like a huge warehouse in comparison to the little camp where we had lived the past four years.

Our cat Sam was yowling all night long at the change in venue. It was a lot to explore for our indoor cat.

Our Dalmatian, Moxie, on the other hand, had spent many an evening with us while we were working on the place and immediately curled up in front of the wood stove and happily went to sleep.

Here I sit enjoying the sun in 2015 with Richard's daughter Christa, who acts as my personal care aide.

I'm off for a sail with Richard and my aide Robin Ward in
2001.

Chapter 25

Renewing Old Acquaintances With a Benefit Barbecue for a Van

One of the first acquisitions Richard bought for the beach house was a sailboat he found locally.

He installed a patio chair for me with the back legs sawed off and I started a new hobby of sailing the lake with Richard.

Although I wasn't as big a fan of sailing as he was, I did enjoy the lake tour. Trouble was, with my penchant for tanning, I always wanted to face the sun and that wasn't always possible with tacking back and forth up and down the lake.

Another of Richard's hobbies was motorcycle

riding and he had bought a Ural motorcycle with a sidecar that had a luggage rack on the back for my folding wheelchair. We spent many happy hours riding, sometimes in a group with the MDA fund-raising rides the local Harley-Davidson dealer sponsored. I often fell asleep in the sidecar, I was so comfortable.

Speaking of fund raisers, my handicapped accessible van that Richard had purchased to handle my wheelchair access was rusting away and needed to be replaced.

So two of my aides, Terry and Kelly, volunteered to put on a fund-raising barbecue to buy me a new (used) accessible van. I also put out the word to my many column readers.

The response was overwhelming. I was able to get a van out of Georgia (where the lack of salt on the roads made car bodies much more resilient over time.) As of this writing I am still using the van almost nine years later! And it was 10 years old when I bought it!

Some of the surprise contributors to the van project included my old landlord, Mike, and my old connection to the acting world, Deborah, whose husband had been Julia Roberts' agent at one time.

See, a new handicapped access van would have cost about $55,000 at the time and that wasn't a possibility. We got this van for a bargain basement price of $13,000. Partly, this was because the computer system that operated the ramp access went bad and in order to get a reduced price, we had the ramp in the floor changed over to manual use and got an extra $1,000 knocked off the price.

Since I wasn't driving, as my hands were no longer working properly, either Richard or my aide would be doing the chauffeuring. Since they were both fully capable, either could work the manual door and ramp.

Speaking of old acquaintances, I had stayed in touch with Mary Woltz in New York City from my days there when I worked with her as well as Michael Chikliss, Edie Falco and Anthony Bourdain all at Formerly Joe's restaurant. She had an apartment on the Upper West Side and we had stayed with her when we attended a concert in NYC.

She came up by train in the winter and we went cross-country skiing at a local resort called Lapland Lake Ski Resort. The place was run by a former Olympic cross-country skier named Olavi (he was from Finland) and he had a special ski-chair I could sit in and Richard could push over the trails. It was a blast feeling like the old downhill days when I used to go skiing with my sister, Mom and Dad. Only this time I didn't fall down as much.

Because of being on the beach, with no obstruction of trees like I had at the camp, I was able to spend a lot more time in the sun and keep up my tan. I could even transfer to my manual chair and be pushed into the shallow water at the beach to enjoy the freedom of movement with the waves and water as an aide or Richard pushed me out in the water.

In the winter, Richard bought me a sun panel to keep up my tan and warm my soul.

With the accessibility of the house, constant view of the water, mountains and sunset (we were on the east shore facing west) and great interior of this Adirondack home, I am more at peace with myself than I had ever been seeking fame and fortune. Funny thing is, I am also better known than I thought would be possible here in the Adirondacks.

As weather watcher for the Albany affiliate of ABC's *News Channel 10* I report daily to chief meteorologist Steve Caporizzo. In fact, in the most recent column I sent in to The Sunday Leader-Herald, I outlined my local notoriety with my name once again "in lights" on TV.

I and Richard sit on our beach in 2007.

Chief Meteorologist Steve Caporizzo displays our view at sunset in Nov. 2015 with my name as weather watcher finally "up in lights."

Chapter 26

A Last Word

This copy of my column for Nov. 15, 2015 seems an appropriate way to end this memoir.

It is how I appear to readers locally in the Sunday newspaper:

Kathryn's Korner Adventures
in Social Media and the Digital Age

So I've been dragged kicking and screaming into the digital world.

I still prefer the old fashioned ways of reading, for instance. Give me a hard back book that Herman has set atop my wooden book holder and I'm a happy camper. Herman tells me he carries a library of eBooks on his little e-reader, but I don't really care.

Still, I've had to make some concessions and grudgingly admit there are some advantages to digital data.

For instance, when I first started writing this column more than 20 years ago, I would print up my copy and FAX it into the newspaper where they had to painstakingly retype it into the computer program for printing. Now I can dictate my column to a word processing program and email it into the newspaper's address where they can edit and copy and print it onto the page.

I know they keep a digital copy of my photo for weekly use and can easily transfer any photos I send with the column.

Today, for instance, I'm gazing at the lake which is still as glass and am sending along a photo Herman took of last night's sunset as it appeared on *News Channel 10's* weather report with Steve Caporizzo.

See, as weather watcher for Caroga Lake, I daily email the temperature and sometimes a relevant weather photo to his email and sometimes it appears on the news. I'm hoping the editors have room on a color page so you can experience the brilliant sunset here as we did. I think weather watchers used to have to telephone information to the TV station.

Then last year an aide got me started on Facebook.

I now have dozens of friends and family all over the country who I can interact with along with photos and videos to see what's going on in their lives.

I've got to experience two long-distance weddings and the arrival of a new grandnephew this way.

And for several years I have sent my column digitally to a list of family and friends out of town by email. That is an especially great way to stay in touch with my extended family in Israel.

If you'd like to be a part of my digital footprint, you'll find me at Kathryn-Phillips Spira on Facebook. Or if you just want to experience my columns the old fashioned way, keep watching this page of The Sunday Leader-Herald!

Kathryn Spira, a native of Cleveland who pursued an acting career in New York City and Los Angeles, now pursues free lance writing from Caroga Lake in Fulton County. Previous columns and contact information may be accessed at her Web site www.kathrynskorner.com

ANGEL CITY TALENT
8228 Sunset Blvd. • 311
Los Angeles, Ca 90046
(213) 650-1930

KATHRYN SPIRA

Height: 5' 6"   Hair: Brown
Weight: 119   Eyes: Brown

FILM

The Doors	Waitress at Whiskey	Oliver Stone, Director
Ghostbusters	Featured	Columbia Pictures
One Woman or Two	Artist	Orion Pictures
The Girls Guide	Co-Star	Six Shooter Films (NYC)

TELEVISION

St. Nicks Flicks	Co-Host	MTV Network, New York
One Life To Live	Day Player	ABC-TV

OFF OFF BROADWAY

Getting Out Of Bed	Melanie	Primary Stages
Sisters of Sisters	Cheryl	American Renaissance Theatre
The Misunderstanding	Maria	Theatre in Action
This Property is Condemned	Willie	Theatre in Action
The Cherry Orchard	Anya	Theatre in Action

REGIONAL & STOCK

American Repertory Theatre		Touring Division
the Mother Goose Odyssey	Mama G.	Cleveland Playhouse & Orchestra
The Wager	Honor	Phoenix Theater Ensemble
Gemini	Judith	Phoenix Theater Ensemble
The Merchant of Venice	Portia	Phoenix Theater Ensemble
Impromptu	Winifred	Cain Park Summer Theatre
A Member of the Wedding	Janice	Cain Park Summer Theatre

TRAINING

Acting: Richard Pinter, NYC (Head of Acting; Neighborhood Playhouse)
               Lev Schectman, (Former Director; Moscow Art Theater) NYC
               Thomas Q. Fulton, Phoenix Theatre Ensemble, Cleveland, Ohio

Voice: Eileen Farrell, Elizabeth Howell

Dance & Movement: Michael Sokoloff, David Morgenstern

SPECIAL SKILLS:

Dialects, Tap Dancer, Swimmer, Printwork, Promotional Modeling, Athlete, Can Drive a Stick Shift

This is a copy of the theatrical resume I would attach to head shots when trying for an acting part or auditioning.

I sit with Richard and our beloved Dalmatian, Moxie, on our beach in Fall 2009.

"See, [as struggling actors]we were always bemoaning our plight as unemployed, under thanked, overworked in "means-to-an-end" jobs while being misunderstood and give me a light for my millionth cigarette as I listen to the blues type.

Who knows?

When I asked Regina if I was ever like that, she stated simply, 'You were worse!'"

— *Kathryn Spira*

Chapter 27

After Word: In Memoriam

There are some people I've lost over the years who have been very important to me.

Joe Spira, my adoptive father who always was supportive of my efforts and whose words, "Nature never clashes," still ring in my ears.

My best friend growing up, Jacques Lorenzo, who first explained the gay experience to me as, "Kathryn, you know how you like boys? Well, so do I. And that's all you need to know about being gay."

My eldest sister, Linda Bliss, who always was encouraging.

My biggest fan, Mike Lewy, who used to make copies of each of my columns for my files and always sent an encouraging note with the copies.

To my Mom, although still alive at this writing, with mid-stage Alzheimer's. We always laughed heartily and who often said, "These are not poor people's problems!" And, "I love you more!"

I sit in the sidecar of Richard's Ural Motorcycle in 2000.